EXPANDING
COLLEGE OPPORTUNITY
a roadmap to college for parents and students

Stanley B. Lemons

Stanley B. Lemons
stanlemons@expandingcollegeopportunity.com
www.expandingcollegeopportunity.com

For bulk orders of *Expanding College Opportunity*, contact
TheSecretToWriting.com at 404.869.1290 or email info@thesecrettowriting.com.

Library of Congress Control Number: 2014917550
ISBN-13: 978-0-9909278-0-8
ISBN-10: 0990927806
Printed in the United States of America

Exterior Design: Erin Hamilton and Cynthia J. Mitchell
Interior Design: Cynthia J. Mitchell
Back Cover Photo by Anderson Flewellen

Expanding College Opportunity is published by The Secret To Writing, LLC.

Contact Information:
The Secret To Writing, LLC
3455 Peachtree Road, N.E., 5th Floor
Atlanta, GA 30326
404.869.1290
info@thesecrettowriting.com
www.thesecrettowriting.com

The
Secret to Writing.com
Because Words Matter

acknowledgements

I want to acknowledge and give special thanks to my family and friends for their love and support in helping me to bring Expanding College Opportunity *to fruition.*

I especially want to thank the following individuals for their encouragement, feedback, and assistance with this book: Tosha Bussey, Larry Chappell, Judith Coleman, Dr. Barbara Graves, Erin Hamilton, Amy Hite, Carver Johnson, Jenine Lemons, Matthew Lemons, Roger Mann, Cynthia J. Mitchell, Joy Mitchell, Marilyn Moody, Jon Nemeth, Shenita Piper, and Ann Rickenbacher Thaxton.

So many people have shown love
for me and invested in my personal
and professional growth…
I am abundantly grateful.

I hope this book, with its markings
of my life journey,
will be a blessing to others.

table of contents

preface

I graduated from Amherst College, a small liberal arts school in Amherst, Massachusetts. Statistically, less than 15% of students who apply to Amherst are admitted.[1]

When I applied to colleges as a high school senior, my goal was simply to go to college. I knew little about Amherst; and, as a first-generation prospective college student, I knew virtually nothing about attending college.

I come from a family of modest financial means, and neither one of my parents attended college. However, like many parents, my mom and dad wanted me to have a good education; in this regard, my story is not uncommon. Students from diverse backgrounds, often in the face of difficult life circumstances, attend and graduate from college.

Yet a problem that many students and parents face is that they are unfamiliar with the college admissions and financial aid processes. This is especially true when the student is the first in his or her family to attend college. (That was certainly the

---

1. 2011-2014 admissions rate data on the Amherst College website

case with mine.) As a result, many students and parents do not know how to take full advantage of the enrollment opportunities available at many colleges or the financial resources that are available to help students attend college.

I wrote *Expanding College Opportunity* to fill that information gap. In my experience leading college seminars for high school students and their families, I've been fortunate to facilitate countless *"I get it"* moments, when students and families understand the process to college admission and financial aid, and realize that they can do this, regardless of their financial or educational background.

With *Expanding College Opportunity,* my goal is to help students realize their dream of going to college. I want you—parents and students—to read *Expanding College Opportunity* and get the information you need—quickly and easily. More than anything else, I want students to embrace the belief: If you want to go to college, you can go. *Expanding College Opportunity* is your roadmap.

My Amherst College Graduation
Left to right:
My brother—Wendell Hart
My mother—Rue Dean Lemons
Me—Stan Lemons
My dad—Walter Lemons

introduction

Expanding College Opportunity is a book that can be used by all students and parents. If a student wants to go to a highly selective college, such as Harvard, Stanford, or Amherst, *Expanding College Opportunity* will provide you with the insight to help you get in. Likewise, if a student wants to attend a local state university, *Expanding College Opportunity* is an equally valuable resource.

Why is going to college important?

There is a great deal of data that supports the answer to this question. Here are my thoughts:

- A college degree provides you with more job or career opportunities during the course of your lifetime
- A college degree helps you earn more money
- The college experience helps you grow as a person by exposing you to new people, new ideas, and new information
- College equips you with the skills and know-how to create new companies or invent new things
- A college degree can help you live a more enjoyable life because you will be in a position to afford an overall higher standard of living

What is the purpose of this book?

The purpose of *Expanding College Opportunity* is as follows:

- To serve as a straight-forward, short, easy-to-read, explanation of the college admissions process
- To ease the anxiety of parents and students about college admissions and paying for college
- To help students gain admission to college

Who is this book for?

- High School Students
- Middle School Students
- Parents
- Educators
- Transfer Students
- International Students

In *Expanding College Opportunity*, I talk primarily to you, the student, although there are parts of the book where I talk directly to parents, educators, and others to address their specific questions and concerns. While you may choose to skip around the sections of *Expanding College Opportunity*, I recommend you read the book from start to finish. I say this because the information in the beginning of the book provides the foundation for some of the points I make later.

There is a lot of information in this book. And while it is my hope that readers will read *Expanding College Opportunity* in its entirety, there are some main points that I hope each constituent group will remember. I share those points with you now.

My main message to high school students:

College admissions officers will review your academic record and extracurricular activities from the beginning of ninth grade through the end of twelfth grade. It is important that you perform at your very best in your classes throughout high school. Having a strong academic record, extracurricular activities, and community involvement will help you to have more college options.

My main message to middle school students:

Middle school prepares you for high school, and ultimately for college. What you do in middle school can set you on a specific path or track in high school. If you perform well in your middle school classes, then your academic record will position you to start high school at a more advanced level. By the time you are a high school junior or senior, you will be in a better position to take advanced-level courses, such as honors or advanced placement classes. The advanced level courses will enhance your academic profile, and likewise benefit you when you get ready to apply to college as a high school senior.

My main message to parents:

Expanding College Opportunity may serve to reacquaint you with the college admissions process, as well as introduce you to new facets of college admissions. For those parents who did not go to college, *Expanding College Opportunity* is intended to familiarize you with the admissions process. After reading this book, you will be in a much better position to help your son or daughter not only get into college, but also to graduate from college.

Expanding College Opportunity also provides information on the fundamentals of the financial aid process. However, *Expanding College Opportunity* is not, nor is it intended to be, a textbook or an all-inclusive manual about college admissions and financial aid. Rather, I provide foundational information. I encourage you to communicate with your child's high school counselors, admissions and financial aid representatives at prospective colleges, and community representatives who work in the field of college admissions for additional information.

My main message to educators:

Consider *Expanding College Opportunity* as your written companion on college admissions and financial aid. The information in this book is intended to reinforce and support the work of high school counselors, teachers, and administrators. I hope school officials will encourage both parents and students to read *Expanding College Opportunity*. *Expanding College Opportunity* will help make the job of educators easier by challenging students to do their very best inside and outside of the classroom, and to pursue higher education.

My main message to transfer students:

…transferring from a two-year college

If you have completed or are soon to complete your associate degree from a two-year college and are now preparing to apply to a four-year college, the topics discussed in *Expanding College Opportunity* will benefit you. For instance, you will need to clearly articulate in your college application to a four-year school why you want to go to a particular college. How have you grown as a person and as a student from your two-year college experience? *Expanding College Opportunity* walks you through the evaluative steps of a college admissions officer at a four-year college.

…transferring from a four-year college

If you are currently at a four-year college and planning to transfer to another four-year college, *Expanding College Opportunity* serves as a refresher to what is involved in the college admissions process. Moreover, admissions officers at the school where you want to transfer will surely want to know and understand your motivation for transferring and how you will contribute to their school community. *Expanding College Opportunity* helps you provide the answers.

My main message to international students:

Now more than ever, there are ample opportunities for international students to study at colleges and universities throughout the United States. U.S. college admissions officers welcome the unique perspectives that international students bring to a college campus since international students enrich the overall academic and social environment.

Expanding College Opportunity provides information that will help you gain admission to U.S. colleges. If you need financial aid to pay for college, you will have to take a more focused approach to identify schools and scholarship programs that offer financial aid to international applicants. Getting into a U.S. college is possible. Getting financial aid to pay for a U.S. college education is also possible. *Expanding College Opportunity* will show you how.

PART 1

the
big picture

**Primary Audience:
All Readers of Expanding College
Opportunity**

CHAPTER 1

overview of the college admissions process

I divide the college admissions process into three simple steps: choose, apply, and decide.

Step 1. Choose
Choose the colleges or universities you would like to attend.

Students need to first and foremost think carefully about their personal goals, learning style, and ambitions, and then consider the type or, as I like to say, the landscape of schools available. Parents or family members can play an important role in helping a student choose where to apply. However, the student, him or herself, is the person who ultimately should choose. Students need to answer the question: what school will be a good fit for me? The goal is to identify schools where you (the student) believe you will be challenged academically, grow as a person, and feel happy.

Step 2. Apply
Submit an application to the schools to which you want to apply.

A college admissions committee—comprised of admissions officers—reviews the information contained in a student's application to determine if the student matches the recruitment goals and priorities of that particular college or university. An admissions committee aims to assemble a unique class of incoming students. In other words, an admissions committee seeks to recruit a class of students that not only can succeed in the classroom, but also students who represent diverse backgrounds, talents, and interests. All these recruitment factors play an important role in the admissions process.

The information included in a student's college application is designed to reflect the cumulative or total academic performance and extracurricular involvement of the student throughout his or her high school years. In this regard, the college admissions process is not an activity that is limited or sidelined to a student's junior or senior years of high school. Rather, the process of applying to college encompasses all four years of high school. For this reason, I strongly encourage both middle school and high school families to begin learning and considering the college admissions process as early as possible. My intent in encouraging families to start planning early for college is not to add to the frenzy, anxiety, or hoopla about college admissions. I simply want to help folks be prepared, make better choices, and avoid unnecessary anxiety or worry.

What are the components of the college application?

The components of the college application include comprehensive information about the student:

- High School Transcript
- Standardized Tests Scores
- Extracurricular Activities
- Recommendations
- Interviews
- Admissions Essays
- Discipline Report (if applicable)

I discuss these components individually in part three of *Expanding College Opportunity*.

Step 3. Decide

Depending on where you are admitted to college, you will need to decide which you want to attend.

The decision about where to enroll or matriculate is based on a student's careful consideration of several factors that make one school versus another feel like a good college fit. The factors grow from a re-consideration of one's goals and ambitions. Ultimately, a student enrolls in one school and later begins his or her college journey at that school.

After a student decides where he or she wants to enroll in college, there are follow-up activities:

- Notify a school of your decision to enr
- Inform the college(s) you decide not t not to enroll
- Continue to perform well in your classes from high school

Once the requirements of a school's application process are complete and a student makes an enrollment decision, then students are essentially done with the college admissions process. If, for example, you are a student-athlete or a student with a special talent, such as an artist, actor, or musician, some colleges may require you to submit additional material or eligibility information about your background. Or, a college may require an audition in the case of a performing artist. But again, after you decide where to enroll (step 3), the admissions process will be complete.

Summary

These three steps—choose, apply, and decide—are the pillars of applying to and getting into college. If you keep these three steps in mind as you prepare to apply to college, the process may seem less intimidating and overwhelming. Yet, as I remind students, the "real work" of the college admissions process starts with the student's classroom performance—from DAY ONE of ninth grade through high school graduation. I can't emphasize this point enough. I repeatedly say to students: if you put forth your best effort in your classes, you will find that getting into and, indeed, getting money to pay for college will be easier.

CHAPTER 2

understanding your college options

Choosing a college to attend should first involve self-analysis and then a consideration of college options. To help give students a foundation to both base their self-analysis and consideration of the many college options, this chapter provides an overview of the college landscape. Let me be candid: some of the information in the chapter is data intensive. And yes, to some readers the data might seem a bit dry to read. However, it is important that you understand the depth and scope of the college landscape in order to fully appreciate the later chapters of the book.

What is the college landscape?

Colleges and universities vary from public and private schools, to community colleges, technical schools and "traditional" four-year schools. Colleges range in size, setting, academic programs, culture, selectivity, and cost.

How many colleges and universities are in the United States?

According to the U.S. Department of Education, there are approximately 7,565 colleges and universities in the United States (2012, Department of Education, Title IV schools. Title IV schools are institutions that receive federal student aid funds).

For clarity, I want to make sure that all readers, particularly young teenagers, of *Expanding College Opportunity* understand the basic differences between a college and a university.

What is a college?

- A college is a school that grants bachelor's degrees and focuses on undergraduate students.
- Most colleges have liberal arts programs. By liberal arts, I mean students study a range of subjects from history, literature, and art to mathematics and the sciences.
- Generally speaking, students earn their college degree in four years.
- Two-year schools, which are commonly referred to as community colleges, grant associate degrees.

What is a university?

- A university grants undergraduate degrees (B.A., B.S. or both) and graduate (M.A., M.S.) or professional (M.D., J.D., M.B.A.) or post graduate degrees (Ph.D.).
- A university is comprised of both undergraduate (or college) students and graduate students. Most undergraduate students enter college within two to three months after graduating from high school. Of course, this is not always the case. Sometimes high school students pursue other endeavors immediately after high school and before starting college, such as working at a job, traveling, or pursuing a military assignment.
- Having completed their undergraduate or college degree,

graduate students choose to study a particular field at a more advanced level.

- Universities grant advanced degrees, ranging from business, law, engineering, computer science or medicine to biology, chemistry, math, history, languages, social sciences, literature, and subjects in the arts.
- The time to complete a graduate degree program ranges from one to six years.

How are colleges and universities categorized? What are examples of each type of school?

I categorize schools into three groups.

Group 1: "Four-year or Traditional Schools"

Public, four-year or above

Examples:

- University of Georgia, Athens, Georgia
- University of California-Los Angeles, Los Angeles, California
- United States Military Academy, West Point, New York

Private not-for-profit, four-year or above

Examples:

- Pepperdine University, Malibu, California
- Bennett College, Greensboro, North Carolina
- Amherst College, Amherst, Massachusetts

Private for-profit, four-year or above

Examples:

- The Art Institute of Austin, Austin, Texas
- University of Phoenix—Northwest Learning Center, Las Vegas, Nevada
- ITT Technical Institute, Akron, Ohio

Group 2: "Two-year or Community Colleges"

Public, two-year

Examples:

- El Centro College, Dallas, Texas
- Santa Monica College, Santa Monica, California
- Butler Community College, El Dorado, Kansas

Private not-for-profit, two-year

Examples:

- Chatfield College, St. Martin, Ohio
- Delaware College of Art and Design, Wilmington, Delaware
- Memorial Hospital School of Nursing, Albany, New York

Private for-profit, two-year

Examples:

- Anthem College—Aurora, Denver, Colorado
- Austin Kade Academy, Idaho Falls, Idaho
- Everest College—Bremerton, Washington

Group 3: "Less than Two-year, Technical, or Trade Schools"

Public, less-than two-year

Examples:

- Culpeper Cosmetology Training Center, Culpeper, Virginia
- Kiamichi Technology Center, Hugo, Oklahoma
- Taylor Technical Institute, Perry, Florida

Private not-for-profit, less-than two-year

Examples:

- Lakeside School of Massage Therapy, Milwaukee, Wisconsin
- Franklin Academy, Cleveland, Tennessee
- Center for Employment Training (CET), Chicago, Illinois

Private for-profit, less-than two-year

Examples:

- Academy of Cosmetology, Richland, Washington
- American Beauty Academy, Wheaton, Maryland
- Arlington Medical Institute, Arlington, Texas

What is the percentage of schools by category?

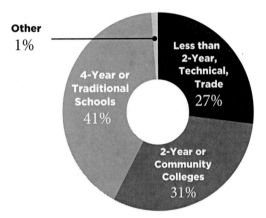

As you can tell from the chart above, four-year colleges represent the largest percentage (41%) of schools. There are approximately 3,101 four-year colleges in the United States. It is these four-year schools that will serve as the bases of much of what I talk about in *Expanding College Opportunity*.

What is the percentage of students in each school category?

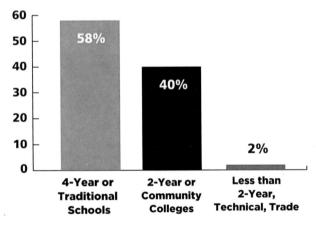

The largest percentage of students (58%) attend four-year institutions. However, the U.S. Department of Education data also reveals that approximately 40% of all U.S. students attend community colleges.

Community colleges are, by definition, geographically accessible to community residents and provide an affordable path to higher education. Many students attend community college for two years, and through "articulation agreements"—primarily with public state schools—these same students are able to transfer to four-year colleges. The "articulation agreements" vary widely from state-to-state and therefore impact the transfer rates from two-year schools to four-year schools.

The fact that approximately 40% of students enroll in community colleges may be a surprise to many people. But in researching colleges in the United States, you will find that community colleges have long been a gateway to higher education for many people, including many national or public figures. According to information obtained from the American Association of Community Colleges website, George Lucas (creator of films, *Star Wars* and *Indiana Jones*), Gwendolyn Brooks (poet and Pulitzer Prize winner), and Nolan Ryan (former baseball pitcher and Baseball Hall of Fame inductee) all attended community college at one point on their path.

While trade and technical schools enroll the smallest percentage of students, the role of these institutions in the higher education landscape is vitally important. Students may choose to attend a trade or technical school after college and enjoy a successful career, for instance, as a welder, barber, electrician, or cosmetologist.

How difficult or selective is it to get into a college?

The average acceptance rate of U.S. colleges and universities is 67% (Department of Education 2012). Stated differently: on average or as a whole, 67% of the applicants who apply to a college are admitted.

How is selectivity defined?

Colleges are often classified into different categories based on their selectivity. The classifications are not scientific or set in stone. One such categorization of college selectivity is found on the bigfuture.collegegboard.org website. Schools are classified in five groups:

- Open Admission (all or most students are admitted)
- Less Selective (> 75% of students are admitted)
- Somewhat Selective (50-75% of students are admitted)
- Selective (25-50% of students are admitted)
- Highly Selective or Most Selective (<25% of students are admitted)

When I talk about selectivity throughout the book, you can use these classifications as a reference.

How much is tuition?

The tuition to attend a college varies from state-to-state and according to the type of institution. The average cost to attend a college might range from $3,000 at a local community college to an average price above $50,000 at some private four-year schools. However, as I discuss in chapter 9, students often do not pay the tuition prices listed on college websites because of the generous opportunities associated with receiving financial aid.

What are the websites for college search databases where you can find detailed information about specific colleges?

www.bigfuture.collegeboard.org

www.collegeweeklive.com

www.nces.ed.gov/collegenavigator

What does the wide range of college options suggest for students?

As a student, you have a wide pool of schools to consider attending. With so many U.S. colleges available to you (not to mention international college options), I know it can be both exciting and overwhelming to choose where to apply. Nonetheless, the decision of where to apply can be simplified by, first and foremost, thinking about what's important to you and what you want your college experience to be like. By thinking in these terms, you will be empowered as a discerning consumer and likewise be in a better position to pick and choose schools that you want to research and ultimately submit an application for admittance.

It is important that you keep the following three points in mind:

- No one school is perfect.
- No school can guarantee you happiness or success in life. And, therefore, there is no reason for you to get stressed out with the notion that you have to get into a few popular or highly selective schools.
- In choosing a college, your main goal should be to identify and apply to schools that you feel good about—places that you think will be a good fit for you.

Now that we've taken a look at the scope and range of the colleges and university landscape, you will have a foundation to understand the next chapter: How to choose a college.

case study - robert

Robert got into several highly selective colleges. Robert was also admitted to a state university not too far from his home. Although Robert's friends thought he should attend one of the highly selective schools, Robert took a different route. Robert chose to attend a local, public college because it was close to home and he could save money by living with his parents. Robert knew he wanted to eventually go to medical school, so he worked hard when he was in college. He earned great grades and was a student leader on campus. For example, Robert was President of the student government and student representative to the Board of Trustees. After college, Robert later applied and was admitted to a top-notch medical school in Baltimore. Today, Robert is a successful pediatric surgeon in Phoenix, Arizona.

thoughts

There is not one road to higher education. Students may attend a public or private school, technical or trade school, or (depending on the circumstances) complete their education through online study. Robert carefully examined his situation and made a thoughtful decision about his college plans and his long-term goals. Robert recognized the significance of not just getting into college, but also performing well while in college. That's exactly what happened with Robert: he earned top grades as an undergraduate student, and as a result Robert is now a proud medical school graduate.

PART 2

making the
college choice

**Primary Audience:
Students**

CHAPTER 3
how to choose a college

So how do you go about choosing a college? It starts with you, the student. What are you like as a person? How would you describe your personality? With these types of questions in mind, you can begin to look at the landscape of colleges and work to identify schools that match your personality and interests.

If you start with considering your personality, goals, and interests, I believe other questions will naturally begin to emerge for you:

- Do you seek to be in a super-competitive classroom environment?
- Are you looking for a more balanced academic and social setting?
- How important is it for you to attend a "prestigious" or "brand name" school?
- Would you like to attend a large university or a small school?
- Would you like to attend a school in an urban setting or in a rural environment?
- Do you want to attend a college that is located out-of-state or a school that is close to home?

These are all questions that require you to do a bit of self-examination in order to answer them. Your answer to these questions will significantly impact the type of school that you might consider attending. In turn, the choice of where you choose to apply to college will be based on careful thought about a good college fit or match for you and not superfluous notions of what's a "good" school.

To further help you with this very important process of self-analysis and choosing where to apply, I include additional questions for you to consider. The following list is not exhaustive, but it should help.

- **Family Tradition**: Do you want to go to a college where your parents or other relatives attended? If you decide to apply where a parent, relative, or friend attended, make sure you are the person who desires to attend the school. What's your gut (or inner voice) telling you? Where you apply to college needs to be a good fit for you—not, for example, a fit for your mom, dad, great uncle, girlfriend or boyfriend, best friend in high school, or anyone else for that matter.

- **Academic Environment**: Do you want to attend a school that places an emphasis on, let's say, mathematics or the performing arts, such as dance, music, or theater? Do you prefer a college that offers programs that are geared toward a particular major (i.e. subject that you want to focus on) or career, such as business, engineering, or medicine? I do realize you might not know. Quite frankly, I think it can be hard for a teenager to know with absolute certainty how he or she wants to spend a long-term career, or where to exactly focus his or her studies in college. Thus, you might think in terms of whether or not a school offers classes in subjects that interest you, as opposed to thinking so much in terms of a specific career. However, if you are set on a particular area of study or career path, you might choose a college that offers a large selection of classes in that subject area.

- **Size**: Would you feel comfortable attending a "small" college where you might be one of 20 students in a class? Or, would you like to attend a college or university where classroom sizes could range from 200 to 300 students? I suggest you think for a moment about where you presently attend high school. Do you want a different learning environment?

- **Co-ed, All-male, or All-female**: Do you think you would focus more on your studies if you attended a single-gender college? Or, do you prefer a mix of men and women in the classroom? If you decide to attend a single-gender college, know that there are often opportunities to take classes at neighboring co-ed institutions. Likewise, a single-gender college may allow students of the opposite gender to enroll in its class(es) as a "visiting" student, in which case you would then have the experience of a co-ed learning environment.

- **Weather**: Like cold weather? Or perhaps it's important for you to live in a warm climate. I wouldn't underestimate the importance of weather on your college experience. Remember: college is where you will live for at least four years. You want to be comfortable.

- **Proximity to Home**: How important is it for you to be close to home? Are you prepared to attend a school located on the other side of the country? What if, for financial reasons, you could only visit home during the summer break? Are you really prepared to only see your family during the summer months or during the holidays? It's a good idea to think seriously about the feasibility and importance to you of being able to visit home while you are a college student. In my case, I made the decision to leave my hometown of Dallas, Texas, to attend a college in Massachusetts. It was not easy at first, but it worked out for me and I'm glad I made that decision. At the same time, the majority of my friends and most students in general stay closer to home to attend college.

- **Special Interest**: Is it important for you to attend a school that is affiliated with a particular religion or set of values? Would you find it empowering to attend a school with a large racial or ethnic community similar to you? Is it important for you to attend a school with a strong reputation for supporting students with disabilities? All of these types of special interests can affect how you feel on a day-to-day basis while in school. And ultimately, these matters can impact how you perform in your classes and the ease in which you are able to build friendships with other students. All these factors are important in shaping your overall college experience.

- **Cost**: Are you applying to schools that vary in cost? Are you considering any schools that are known to offer substantial financial aid packages? Would attending a community college be a good starting point for you? I know that the cost of college is a big consideration for many people. Dare I say that cost should be an important consideration when applying to college? Let me also say that cost, as I talk about in Part Five of *Expanding College Opportunity*, should not stop you from applying to a school. You should apply to any college that you desire to apply to even if you think the college is unaffordable. Many schools offer substantial financial aid packages that include scholarships and grants, so that you can go to school without having to pay much, nor take out substantial loans. Again, I am going to go into greater detail about paying for college later in the book.

As you think about the aforementioned points on choosing a college, I strongly encourage you to keep notes about your thoughts. Writing down your feelings and aspirations about the type of school you want to apply to will help you stay organized and provide you with a benchmark to refer to when making your final decision on where to attend.

Left: *My mother and me during my first year of college. When I went away to college, I traveled by myself. My mother visited me during Parents Weekend of my freshman year. She later returned to the college four years later for my college graduation.*

Below: *At our college football game during Parents Weekend. Left to right: Professor John A. Petropulos (my college advisor), my mother, and me.*

exhibit 1

Key Considerations When Applying to College

Factors to Consider	Level of Importance
• Size	1 2 3 4 5 6 7 8 9 10
• Setting (Urban, rural, big city, college town)	1 2 3 4 5 6 7 8 9 10
• Location (In-state, out-of-state)	1 2 3 4 5 6 7 8 9 10
• Family Ties to the School	1 2 3 4 5 6 7 8 9 10
• Academic Rigor	1 2 3 4 5 6 7 8 9 10
• Academic Offerings (Liberal arts, technical subjects, performing arts)	1 2 3 4 5 6 7 8 9 10
• Gender (Co-ed, all-male, all-female)	1 2 3 4 5 6 7 8 9 10
• Weather	1 2 3 4 5 6 7 8 9 10
• Proximity to Home	1 2 3 4 5 6 7 8 9 10
• Religious Affiliation	1 2 3 4 5 6 7 8 9 10
• Cultural or Ethnic Affiliation	1 2 3 4 5 6 7 8 9 10
• Support Services	1 2 3 4 5 6 7 8 9 10
• LGBT Friendly (Lesbian, gay, bisexual, and transgender)	1 2 3 4 5 6 7 8 9 10
• Fraternities, Sororities, or Other Social Outlets	1 2 3 4 5 6 7 8 9 10
• Housing Options	1 2 3 4 5 6 7 8 9 10
• Cost (But remember, don't let cost stop you from applying to a college. With financial aid, you may end up paying little to no money to attend a school.)	1 2 3 4 5 6 7 8 9 10

After you rate the factors in the table, highlight the considerations that you gave the highest score. The considerations with the highest score are the factors that you should pay special attention to when considering and ultimately choosing where to apply to a college.

case study - michael

Michael was an All-American basketball point-guard. To top it off, he was a scholar...salutatorian of his high school class. Michael was admitted to every college where he applied. His big question was: where would he enroll?

Michael decided on a Catholic school located in Washington D.C. He chose the school for three reasons: its academic reputation, its premier basketball program and nationally known coach, and its emphasis on the academic success of student-athletes. Michael definitely hoped to play pro basketball in the NBA, though he also carefully weighed the uncertainty of being drafted. Michael knew there would be life after basketball. That said, Michael felt the college he selected needed to be a great place to play college basketball, but more importantly, the college need be a great place to get a good education.

thoughts

College is and should be, first and foremost, about academics. You read, write, and do math in college. Reading, writing, and mathematics are fundamental components of going to college. In Michael's case, his education will undoubtedly help him to be a critical thinker, and no doubt a strategic player on the basketball court. Michael's college education will serve him well for his entire life.

CHAPTER 4

researching colleges

In this chapter, I talk about how to research colleges and how to develop a list of prospective colleges to which you may apply. Today, students are fortunate to have a number of research resources available. From the information on the internet and in libraries to the advice that comes from family, friends, counselors and mentors, I hope you will take advantage of these resources. But I also hope you will seriously take the time to think and reflect on yourself and what you want to get out of college, as well as the type of college experience you seek to have. Self-analysis and reflection is an important part of the college admissions process and should be done alongside, if not way before, your research on colleges. That said, let's talk about researching colleges.

What are ways you can learn about a college?

- Visit colleges. If you can visit a school, then you will be able to get a better feel for the type of college that is most appealing to you. Students typically visit colleges during their sophomore and junior years of high school. The visits often happen during the spring or summer breaks and on weekends throughout the year.

- If, for whatever reason, you are not able to visit a college that you are interested in attending, you can use the internet—at your home, public library, or some other facility—to learn about a school. Thanks to technology and the internet, you can take a "virtual" or cyber tour of many colleges.

- Keep in mind that you can also visit a college in your local community. Even if you are not interested in attending that particular college, there is tremendous value in getting onto a college campus. You can see what a college classroom looks like and in some cases sit in on a class. You can also check out what students do during their free time, such as socializing in the student center or relaxing at student social areas. Finally, you might benefit from seeing what college buildings and recreation facilities look like.

- College fairs, which are customarily FREE of charge, provide another great way to learn about a college. The National Association for College Admission Counseling (NACAC) publishes a list of college fairs throughout the United States. View the NACAC website at www.nacacnet.org to learn about college fairs in your area.

- Friends and family members can be another important source of information. But let me point out: if you talk with a family member about a school that that person attended, the individual may be biased (positively or negatively). Remember: a friend or family member's experience at a college is, in and of itself, neither good nor bad. It is their experience… one person's perspective about a school. Keep this point in mind as you get feedback and don't let one person's views shape your opinion about a college.

case study - jenine

Jenine participated in Upward Bound. Upward Bound helped Jenine develop a sense of purpose for herself and her studies. Consequently, Jenine's high school grades showed a trend of improvement as she progressed through high school. Anyone who observed Jenine could easily see she was a bright and highly motivated student. When it came to deciding on a college, Jenine had several options. Jenine, who, by the way, is African American, decided to enroll in a Historically Black College (HBCU). She felt that an HBCU would be a good college fit. Additionally, Jenine also wanted to attend a liberal arts college for women. Jenine chose Bennett College in Greensboro, North Carolina.

thoughts

Jenine recognized the importance of a good college fit. Jenine considered the strong academic reputation of Bennett, and likewise other factors that would impact her ability to perform well in college and to graduate on time. Jenine wanted a supportive environment, one that would help her to be successful. Jenine found an ideal school for her…Bennett College.

How many schools should you research?

There is not a prescribed number of schools to research. The number could be 25, 50, 100 or more. From a manageability standpoint, you will probably want to narrow your list of prospective colleges that you want to research extensively to 10-20 schools.

High school counselors, parents, or mentors can help with developing your college list. I know it is not an easy task to develop a list of prospective colleges, but having a prospective list or "basket" of schools that you would be happy to attend is a critical step in the admissions process.

How do you narrow your prospective college list to places where you want to apply?

Make sure your list of prospective schools includes places where you have a strong chance or high probability of being admitted. One way to assess your candidacy for admission is to look at a college's website and review the admissions statistics and profiles of students who have been recently admitted. That said, I caution you to not rely solely on the admitted student profiles you find on websites. (Remember, college websites are often large advertisements.) What you see on a college's website may only represent a small percentage of admitted students. If you are strongly interested in a particular college, talk with your college counselor, an alumnus of the school, or an admissions representative at that school to find out how your background fits with the school.

What if someone tells you not to go to a school or you won't be admitted into a particular college?

Sometimes good-hearted and well-meaning people may advise you not to apply to a particular school. These same advisors may not have any malicious intent by discouraging you to apply to a college that you are interested in. In fact, there may very well be a legitimate reason why a college may not be a good fit for you. With all that said, I believe you must also remember that you are in control of where you choose to apply to college or not to apply. I want you to keep the following point in mind: until you apply to a college and receive an answer from an admissions officer, nobody knows with 100% certainty if you will be admitted or denied admission to a college. I know plenty of students who wanted to apply to a certain school, but did not apply because the student was discouraged from applying based on frivolous or unsubstantiated reasons. I think you just have to be open to listen to the advice of others and likewise not be afraid to get a second (or third) opinion if something doesn't feel right to you.

Additionally, I encourage students to have confidence in themselves and be open to applying to schools that they may not have previously considered. Counselors should be able to give you feedback on how your background fits with the profile of students at a particular college. But just remember, you (the student) are in control of where you choose to apply.

exhibit 2

For illustrative purposes, consider the criterion I use to develop a hypothetical prospective list or "basket" of ten schools to apply to:

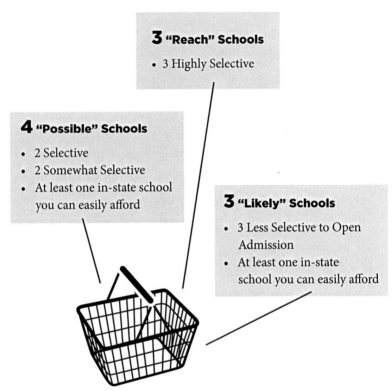

3 "Reach" Schools

- 3 Highly Selective

4 "Possible" Schools

- 2 Selective
- 2 Somewhat Selective
- At least one in-state school you can easily afford

3 "Likely" Schools

- 3 Less Selective to Open Admission
- At least one in-state school you can easily afford

Selectivity Ranges

- Open Admission (all or most students are admitted)
- Less Selective (> 75% of students are admitted)
- Somewhat Selective (50-75% of students are admitted)
- Selective (25-50% of students are admitted)
- Highly Selective or Most Selective (<25% of students are admitted)

Source: www.bigfuture.collegegboard.org

What to do when there's conflict between parents and students about the college admissions process?

I address this question by first making the general statement: the college admissions process can be highly emotional. Students may feel anxious about being accepted or denied admission. Parents, understandably, may sometimes transfer their hopes and dreams for their child onto the student's college search. If, for instance, a student's approach to the college admissions process is different—dare I say opposite—from a parent's approach, then both the student and the parent may find themselves in conflict. Herein is where things can get stressful.

I encourage parents and students to maintain an ongoing dialogue about prospective college lists and the admissions process in general. Communicate. As I've suggested earlier, the student is the person who needs to be proactive in choosing a college. Students, as I say, should feel a sense of personal responsibility for their college search. Once you (the student) actually start at a college, then you will be the person who is accountable for going to class and doing the work. If you feel positive about where you are attending school, there is a greater chance you will perform better in school, enjoy your college years, and graduate on time.

What are possible outcomes if a student attends a college that is not a good fit?

To address this question, I ask you to consider the following possible outcomes:

- The student feels miserable.
- It may take longer to graduate, thereby increasing the overall cost of your college education.
- The student may not perform well in school. In the same way that having good grades help to get into college, good grades help to get a job or gain admittance to graduate or professional schools after college.
- The student may not develop healthy relationships with fellow college students. A large part of the college experience involves building peer relationships. These relationships often lay the foundation for future professional ties or networks. If a student is happy with his or her college environment, then that student may find it easier to form positive relationships with fellow students.
- The student may drop out of college.

Hopefully, these outcomes solidify in your mind the importance of carefully thinking about where you want to apply to school.

Finally, I want you to consider another point that underscores the importance of college fit. Consider: the graduation rate of students at four-year colleges is approximately 59% (This figure is based on U.S. Department of Education data that reflects the graduation rates of full-time, first-time students entering a 4-year college in 2005 and graduating within six years.) There are numerous factors that influence college graduation rates. But, I will say, the topic of college fit, in combination with financial issues, is an important factor in the graduation data. While there is steady work and progress taking place to improve the graduation rate of students in the U.S., I am certainly hopeful that the number will move toward a speedy upward trend. But, not to worry. If you follow a systematic process of self-analysis and research that I have been discussing thus far, both applying and gaining admission into a college that is a good fit is within reach.

What if you want to transfer?

There are plenty of cases in which a student enrolls in a college and for a host of reasons decides to transfer to a different school. Transferring is perfectly fine. There is nothing wrong with making a change for what you believe will be a better situation for you. However, I advise students who seek to transfer to be clear about their reasons for wanting to transfer. There are plenty of options that a student might consider in lieu of or before transferring, such as seeking counseling to directly address an issue, going abroad as an exchange student, or attending another college as a visiting student. Moreover, a student may experience a period of "homesickness" when starting college, especially during the first semester of the first year. If a student starts to think about transferring to a different college during the first semester of school, I would encourage him or her to try to give it some time before making a change.

PART 3

getting
into college

**Primary Audience:
Students**

CHAPTER 5

grades, standardized tests, extracurricular activities

The components covered in this chapter and, for the most part, the remaining chapters of *Expanding College Opportunity* assume you (the student) are applying to a four-year college or an undergraduate program at a university. I use the term college generically, referring to both a college and an undergraduate program at a university.

What do colleges look for in an applicant?

Grades

Grades are fundamental to college admissions. College admissions officers often say: your performance in high school is the main predictor of your success in college. Therefore, keep the following points in mind:

• Take your classes seriously from DAY ONE of high school. Do your best. That means you must put forth 100 percent effort in your classes. All students may not get "A's", but all students have the ability to put forth their best effort and to get help (from free tutoring offered at school to studying in peer groups) in order to earn higher grades.

- Admissions officers like to see an upward trend in grades. If, for example, your freshman year grades are not so good, it is important that you demonstrate improvement in your grades as you progress through high school.

- Junior and senior year grades are reviewed with special emphasis by college admissions officers. Why? College admissions officers presume you will develop and mature as a high school student. Further, admissions officers presume you will focus more on your schoolwork as you get older. The increased focus on doing well in your classes tends to naturally result in higher grades. What does this all mean? Simply stated: put forth your best effort from DAY ONE of high school and you will position yourself to have more college options.

- Colleges like you to complete core courses. Those core courses may include 4 years of math, 4 years of language arts, 3-4 years of science, 3-4 years of a "foreign" or world language, and 3-4 years of social studies. This list of course requirements is just one scenario of needed classes. Look at a college's website to see what type of courses are recommended. In the United States, there are state guidelines that outline courses that students need to successfully complete in order to graduate from high school. The graduation requirements of your high school are aligned with state curriculum requirements. Nevertheless, there are cases in which I learned of high school seniors who approach their high school graduation without having satisfied their school's graduation requirements. Unfortunately, these students will often not graduate from high school on time.

How can you avoid the scenario of not being able to graduate? Make sure you have the requisite or correct classes to graduate from your high school. And, make sure the classes you take in high school will be welcomed, or even expected, by the types of colleges where you might apply. It helps if you take some time, as early as 7th or 8th grade, to view college websites and look for the type of courses that a particular school expects you to complete in high school.

- Most colleges look favorably on the successful completion of Honors or Advanced Placement (AP) classes. Success in an Honors or AP class illustrates a student's desire to challenge him or herself. However, the completion of Honors or AP classes is no guarantee of admission. In most cases, it is more impressive for you to earn, let's say an "A", in a standard level class versus a "D" or "C" in an AP class.

While there are a number of components that admissions officers review when considering an applicant, academic performance, in conjunction with the rigor of your classes, serves as the most important component of your college application. Admissions officers want to feel confident that you can do the academic work at their college and graduate.

Standardized Tests

Standardized test scores from the SAT Reasoning Test (SAT) or the ACT are yet another part of the college admissions process. Standardized tests are generally three hours in length and aim to provide an assessment of a student's academic readiness for college level work. Because students attend different types of high schools, standardized tests are intended to provide a common measurement among applicants, even applicants from outside the United States.

Still, standardized tests are only one element—albeit an important one—in the college admissions process. You should do your best on standardized tests. However, it is not productive for students and (for that matter their parents) to stress about standardized tests. I recommend that you take the SAT or ACT (and in some cases SAT Subject Tests) at the end of junior year. Get a score. Keep it moving. If you choose to retake a standardized test then do so. Many colleges will "superscore" or take the highest score of any given section of a standardized test. However, I recommend you only take a standardized test twice, and only a third time if you truly believe you can inprove your score. Your score may not improve that significantly if you take a standardized test more than three times. You might be better served by focusing your time and energy on your classes, as well as extracurricular activities.

Are there colleges that do not require standardized tests?

Yes. There are a growing number of four-year colleges that do not require standardized tests as part of their admissions criterion. View www.fairtest.org for a list of these test optional schools.

What is included on the SAT and ACT?

Standardized tests generally include a reading, mathematics, and sometimes a science section. As of 2005, the administrators of the ACT and SAT added a writing component to their respective standardized tests. The writing section tests your knowledge of grammar and your ability to communicate effectively in writing.

SAT Subject Tests

SAT Subject Tests are another form of standardized testing that many colleges, especially highly selective schools, require students to take. The SAT Subject Tests are one hour in length and are designed to assess a student's knowledge of a particular subject, such as literature, science, history, math, and "foreign" languages.

When researching colleges, you should be sure to find out which standardized tests are required by a particular school. Standardized testing information is typically found in the admissions section of a college's website. One testing strategy for students is to take SAT Subject Tests near the time you complete that same subject in high school; in that way, the information on the SAT Subject Test will be fresh in your mind.

How do you prepare for standardized tests?

To prepare for standardized tests, students should read as much as possible. Read a wide variety of texts, including novels, non-fiction books, newspapers, magazines, short stories, poems, and even blogs. As you've probably heard on many occasions, reading is fundamental. The more you read, the better you will perform in school and the better you will perform on standardized tests.

If you are not a fan of reading, then I suggest you try reading topics that truly interest you. For example, if you like sports, then read sports material. Read magazines, newspaper articles, or biographies about athletes. There is a lot to say for reading a wide range or varied subjects (and I hope you do). I happen to think you will be a more knowledgeable and interesting person if you develop an interest in a range of topics. But, in keeping with the purpose of this book, my main concern is that you read.

Arithmetic, algebra, and geometry are the core math skills tested on the ACT and SAT. Doing well in your math classes in high school will help you on the math section of standardized tests.

Should you take a Standardized Test Preparatory Course?

Today, it is common practice for students to enroll in preparatory courses for the SAT and ACT. I recommend test preparation classes for students. Having a structured program can help you study more effectively and often times acquaint you with test-taking tips and strategies. However, enrolling in a fee-based standardized testing course is not an absolute requirement to do well on standardized tests. You can utilize FREE test preparation resources available to you on the internet or at your local public library. The key to doing well on standardized tests is to start preparing early. You must (1) have the discipline to study for the tests, and (2) start studying early enough to gain a thorough understanding of the various tests' formats and requirements.

How might changes to standardized tests impact students?

Standardized testing companies, such as the College Board (the company that designs and administers the SAT) and ACT, Inc. (the company that creates the ACT) periodically make changes to standardized tests to address trends in education and the needs of students. Should parents and students fret about the changes or any potential changes to the standardized tests? Absolutely not.

The companies that produce the standardized tests do a good job of communicating information to the public about what's to come with the tests, as well as making available review guides to help students prepare for the tests. I recommend you and your parents to stay abreast of any future changes to the SAT or ACT by viewing the respective websites associated with each exam. Visit www.collegeboard.org for the SAT and SAT Subject Tests. Visit www.act.org for information about the ACT. More importantly, a fail-safe way to prepare for standardized tests, irrespective of their current or future format, is to do well in your high school classes. The ability to read, write, analyze data, and solve math problems will equip you with the skills to do well on standardized tests.

How much do standardized tests cost? When are standardized tests offered? How do you register for standardized tests?

The answer to these questions, along with a complete schedule of when and where the tests are offered can be found by visiting the SAT and ACT websites.

Which standardized test should you take?

Most colleges give you the option to take either the ACT or the SAT. (And again, www.fairtest.org lists schools that do not require standardized tests.) Review the standardized test requirements of the schools to which you want to apply in order to know which tests to take for that particular school.

Take practice tests for both the SAT and the ACT. The test that you consistently score the highest on will be the test you want to most focus on—assuming the colleges where you want to apply accept that particular test.

What if you cannot afford to pay for a standardized test?

Not to worry. Visit www.collegeboard.org and www.act.org in order to view information on how to obtain a fee waiver. You can also talk with your high school counselor about obtaining a fee waiver.

The PSAT and PLAN

As part of the preparation for the SAT and ACT, high school counselors may offer students the Preliminary Scholastic Aptitude Test (PSAT) and PLAN. The PSAT provides formal practice for the SAT. PLAN provides formal practice for the ACT. Students generally take the PSAT and PLAN during their high school sophomore or junior year or both years. The tests are usually administered at your high school, or one nearby.

The PSAT and PLAN are not required for college admissions. The tests are for practice purposes. They do help identify subject areas that may need attention prior to the SAT and ACT.

The PSAT, in particular, enables you to be considered for a National Merit Scholarship. (In fact, a more formal name for the PSAT is the Preliminary SAT/National Merit Scholarship Qualifying Test). The National Merit Scholarship Corporation awards money for college studies based on a student's PSAT score and high school academic performance. To learn more about the National Merit Scholarship Program, view www. nationalmerit.org.

case study - margaret

Margaret attended a small, rural high school of 250 students in Topeka, Kansas. She took a rigorous course load in high school and was involved in her community. As a child, Margaret was nicknamed..."fish"... because of her love for the water. Margaret wanted to study marine biology in college and eventually get a job as an aquatic animal behavior scientist.

Margaret hoped to leave her hometown in Kansas and attend a school in Florida. She was admittedly nervous about applying to Florida schools, as she thought the Florida colleges would not want a girl from a small public high school in the Midwest. Fortunately, Margaret had a wonderful family-friend and mentor, Mr. Lamont. Mr. Lamont encouraged Margaret to "reach for the stars" and apply to a range of colleges, including one local state university in Kansas. (The local state university would serve as a "likely" school for Margaret.) Margaret applied to ten colleges, one in Kansas and nine in Florida. She was admitted to seven schools, denied admission at two, and wait-listed at one school. Margaret went to Florida and is now studying Marine Science/Biology.

thoughts

Margaret worked hard in high school. She took advantage of the resources available to her and had the courage to pursue her dreams of leaving the state and going to Florida. In terms of selectivity, Margaret applied to places that she considered to be "likely" schools, "possible" schools, and "reach" schools. The Florida admissions officers welcomed the geographical diversity of having a student from the Midwest. Unbeknownst to Margaret, college admissions officers work exceedingly hard to recruit a diverse class of students. Why? Diversity among students is at the root of a dynamic and relevant learning environment. Most, if not all, colleges seek diversity.

case study - james

James, a.k.a. "Jimmy", was concerned about paying for college. He considered attending community college, and debated whether or not to apply to public four-year universities or private four-year colleges.

thoughts

Community college is a great option for James. James should also consider applying to four-year colleges. He could receive substantial financial aid from a four-year school. In fact, the cost for James to attend a four-year college may be lower than attending a community college, or a technical or trade school. James needs to remember to consider a "basket" of schools in terms of admissions selectivity and cost. James should definitely not let the cost of a college stop him from applying.

Extracurricular Activities

Participation in extracurricular activities can show that you are a well-rounded student, as well as someone who is willing to contribute to the community in which you live.

Students ask: in which extracurricular activities should I participate? There is no right or wrong answer. You might:

- Play on a sports team
- Volunteer in your community
- Write for the school newspaper
- Work at a job in your field of interest

What's important is your level of involvement and your commitment to the extracurricular activity. Admissions officers like to see an application that identifies a student who pursued his or her true interest or passion during high school. Further, the number of extracurricular activities you are involved in is far less important than both the quality and depth of your experiences in those activities.

You might explore different types of extracurricular activities when you are a freshman and sophomore in high school. If possible, I suggest you continue with one or two of the activities as you progress through your junior and senior years of high school. By pursuing one or two activities throughout high school you will undoubtedly grow in both experience and knowledge of the activity. Likewise, your commitment to a few select activities creates a greater opportunity for you to develop your leadership skills, a valuable asset in the college admissions process.

When the time comes to fill-out your college applications, you will need to list your extracurricular activities on your application and explain what you did.

Here are sample questions about extracurricular activities that you will find on many college applications:

- In what activity did you participate?
- When did you participate in the activity?
- What was your role?
- What were your accomplishments?
- In what way did you grow from your participation in the activity?

As you can see from these questions, there is value in having taken notes about your activities throughout high school. You can easily forget details. I encourage students to jot down in a notebook or journal their reflections or feelings about an extracurricular activity. Keep your notes in a file. Even if you end up storing the file until your senior year, then you will have the notes to refer back to.

Participate in extracurricular activities that you enjoy. Don't try to manipulate the college admissions process by doing activities with the sole intent of wanting to impress a college admissions committee. Getting involved in activities that have meaning to you will be more enriching for you and consequently help you grow as both a student and person. Growth and personal development are the very attributes that college admissions officers like to see in applicants.

CHAPTER 6

recommendations, interviews, admissions essays, discipline report

I continue the discussion about what admissions officers look for in an applicant by reviewing the following: recommendations, interviews, admissions essays, and the discipline report.

Recommendations

Colleges typically require you to provide two to three letters of recommendation. The recommendations serve to provide insight about you as a student and as a person.

Admissions officers include in the college application specific guidelines as to who might write a recommendation for you. Your high school teachers—often times junior or senior year teachers—are the most common writers of letters of recommendation. However, a teacher from your freshman or sophomore year of high school could possibly write a recommendation for you.

Students provide their recommender(s) with a college's recommendation form (including an envelope with a stamp). You will most likely be asked on the recommendation form if you wish to waive or give up your right to read the recommendation. In almost all cases, it is a good idea to say yes or waive your right to see a recommender's evaluation. By having the completed recommendation form remain confidential (between the writer and a college's admissions committee), there is greater latitude for a recommender to write a more honest and candid evaluation. College admissions officers want this type of authentic feedback about a student.

Recommenders are asked to comment on the following:

- How you performed in class?

  (Performance includes not only your grade in a class, but also and equally important, the effort you put forth in a class. Sometimes a recommendation from a teacher who can speak favorably about your strong work ethic can have more weight or influence than a recommendation from a teacher in whose class you earned a high grade.)
- How motivated are you as a student?
- How did you contribute to the overall class?
- How do you interact with peers?
- How might you perform in a college environment?

With this list of potential questions a recommender might be asked, I advise students to do the following:

- Establish and maintain a positive, respectful teacher-student relationship with all your teachers. Your interactions with others both in and outside the classroom not only reflects on your maturity and development, but also is an important factor in shaping the quality of future letters of recommendation.

- Ask people who really know you well to write a recommendation on your behalf. Avoid trying to impress an admissions officer by asking someone "famous" to write about you, particularly if that person doesn't know you well. College admissions officers want to know you.

- Ask people who you think will be enthusiastic about writing a positive recommendation for you. You might ask your potential recommender if he or she would feel comfortable writing a recommendation on your behalf. If the person declines or gives you a lukewarm response, then ask someone else. I would believe that if you are a respectful and hard-working student during your high school years, you will find teachers, counselors, and mentors to be more than happy and willing to write a highly supportive recommendation on your behalf.

- Update your recommenders on your past or current coursework and extracurricular activities. You might provide a recommender with a copy of your transcript or previous report card, résumé, a description of your community involvement, or a list of your extracurricular activities. This information will refresh the memory of your recommenders about you. Some recommenders may not ask for nor want supporting material, but others may find the information to be helpful. Recommenders can use the data from the material you provide as a reminder of your strengths and contributions, as well as specific, concrete examples of your contributions.

- Ask your potential recommenders early about writing a letter on your behalf. Ideally, I encourage students to ask a potential recommender to write on your behalf in the late spring of your junior year. At the latest, a student might talk with a potential recommender in August or early September of your senior year. Why is this so important? Recommenders need enough time to write an effective letter of recommendation. Some recommenders might also be overloaded with requests from students to write letters of recommendation, and consequently the recommender may not be able to write for you. As such, it will serve you well if you give a recommender as much advanced notice as possible, as well as a list of all the schools to which you plan to apply and the corresponding school's application deadlines.

The Counselor Recommendation

Admissions officers ask high school counselors to complete a recommendation letter, sometimes referred to as a secondary school report. Because counselors are typically not in the classroom with students, the counselor's recommendation plays a different role. Counselors explain a high school's curriculum, and consequently are able to illuminate how a student performed in the context of a particular school environment.

A counselor can also explain any extenuating or special circumstances that may have impacted your performance in high school. Extenuating circumstances can involve more personal information, such as:

- The death or illness of a family member that significantly impacted a student's performance
- A medical condition that may have impacted a student
- A family situation that may have impacted a student
- Unusual demands on a student's time and energy

As you can see, the role of a high school counselor is important. I, therefore, strongly recommend that you talk with your school counselor as often and honestly as possible.

If you attend a high school with a large number of students, I recognize that it can be a challenge to casually meet with counselors. However, you may schedule appointments. If you are denied an appointment, have your parent(s) make an appointment, and make sure you attend, with a written list of questions.

Don't get worried or too preoccupied about not being able to meet regularly with your counselor. Unfortunately, there is just a limited number of counseling resources available in almost all schools. But you have other ways of getting college counseling support (like reading this book). Moreover, college admissions officers are aware and understand situations of limited counseling resources available in most schools. College admissions officers have other channels for getting the information needed to review your application.

In almost all cases, a college admissions officer will receive a profile of your high school. As well, an admissions officer will do his or her own research about your school, and undoubtedly will be able to assess your high school performance.

Finally, I want you to also know that a specific category or type of high school, such as a public school, private school, or boarding school does not, categorically speaking, give a student an advantage in the admissions process. College admissions officers will evaluate your application in the context of your high school and your performance in that school.

Interviews

Some colleges offer students admissions interviews. At the same time, a good number of schools do not offer interviews. An increase in the number of applicants and the issue of time (or the lack thereof) to interview applicants are principle reasons why many colleges today do not offer in-person interviews.

With that said, I want you to keep the following points in mind: If you do have an interview, treat the interview as a huge opportunity. It's an opportunity to learn new information about a college. Take a list of questions with you. However, I suggest you try to ask questions that are not readily available on a college's website, such as:

- What type of study abroad programs are available?
- How would you describe the academic advising system?

- What is the graduation rate of students? And, what resources are available to help students be successful, as well as ensure that students graduate?
- What types of school-sponsored events happen on the weekends?
- How do you foster diversity and inclusion at your school?
- What type of college-sponsored scholarships are available?

Be prepared to be asked a series of questions before you are given the opportunity to ask questions. You can Google potential college interview questions and practice your answers.

An interview is an opportunity to make a favorable impression on an admissions officer. Here are a few tips:
- Take the interview seriously.
- Research a college.
- Think about questions you want to ask prior to the interview.
- Allow someone to interview you so you can practice your interview.
- Be polite.

If a college does not offer interviews, you can connect with a school's admissions officers in other ways:

- By going to a college fair and talking with a college's representative
- Reaching out to an alum of the school in your area
- Contacting the school via phone or email to ask questions

By being proactive in contacting a school official or representative, you will indirectly communicate an interest in the college. Admissions officers describe this type of communication from applicants as demonstrated interest. Depending on the college, demonstrated interest can be a pivotal factor in the admissions process.

Admissions Essays

The majority of colleges, particularly private colleges, require at least one but often three to five admissions essays. You might have to prepare one to two 500 word essays (approximately two typewritten, double spaced pages in length), and a shorter set of supplemental essays of approximately one paragraph to one page. Admissions essays are a critical component of the application process. Your response to the essay questions enables admissions officers to get to know you by the way you express yourself in writing. If you are applying to a highly selective college, in which case the vast majority of applicants have similarly high standardized test scores and superior high school grades, the college admissions essay can play an especially important role in differentiating you from other applicants and ultimately gaining admission to a school.

I know that writing college admissions essays may not be the most exciting activity. In fact, college admissions essays can be quite unnerving for many students. But it doesn't have to be that way. I want you to view college admissions essays and scholarship application essays as an opportunity to tell your story.

Here are seven tips to help you write your college admissions essays:

1. Answer the question.
2. Follow the guidelines, i.e. word count or page length.
3. Write well.
4. Proofread your essay. And have someone else who is a "good writer" proofread your essay.
5. Make your essay personal: tell your story. No matter your topic, illustrate what you have learned, and add key details to bring life to your story.
6. Be clear about what you want the essay to reveal about you. In other words, how do you want an admissions officer to feel or view you as an applicant after reading your essay?
7. Use the grandma or grandpa test. If your grandparents were to read your essay, would they be offended or embarrassed? If you suspect the answer to this question is yes, then get feedback from a teacher or counselor about your choice of topic. Feedback from another person will help you think through your ideas.

Students often read books filled with sample college admissions essays. Admissions essay books can be helpful by offering you a perspective on the range of topics students choose to write about, as well as how a student might approach an essay topic. However, the essays of other people should not define how and what you write about in your essay. I reiterate here: college admissions officers want to know you. Admissions officers want to hear your story. What's important to you? What challenges have you faced? How have you dealt with success or failure? And ultimately, how have you grown as a student and as a person?

When I started to write *Expanding College Opportunity*, I reviewed one of my college admissions essays. The essay, or more precisely the experience I recount in the essay, is personal. It's part of my story. It represents a major, or as it were, a life-changing experience.

In re-reading my essay now—as an adult—I felt strong emotions about what I wrote in my college essay. What do I mean? It was as if I were 17 years old again. In my room. At my desk. Writing. Scared and nervous about sharing my inner thoughts. Wondering how my words would be interpreted. Yet, I felt the call to bring a college admissions officer into my world.

My college admissions essay question required that I write about a special experience that had meaning to me. Here is what I said.

– Personal Experience –

"Private school—are you kidding, man? I don't wan' go to no school with all those white kids! They all stuck up! Anyway, private school is too hard and my mama can't afford it anyhow."

Did I really say this? Is it possible?
Seven years ago maybe I really did.

I was shooting basketball seven years ago in the gymnasium of the Oak Cliff Boys' Club. The Boys' Club was a place that endeavored to guide boys, especially boys from low-income families, in mental, vocational, and social standing, as well as character development. However, in my mind, these things didn't apply to me. I had already planned to play Pro basketball and my morality was just fine. The only reason I went to the Boys' Club was for the inside gym that it had.

Martha, the librarian at the club and a good friend of mine, approached me while I was in the middle of a game of one-on-one with Spud (I didn't know his real name, but everybody called him that). Martha told me about a private school that I hadn't even heard of called Greenhill. She said that the school was giving admission tests and she thought I should apply. Well, naturally, I thought that was out of the question:

none of my friends had ever gone to a private school. A few days passed, and every day Martha would pester me about the school. Finally, I gave in and agreed to take the test.

I remember waking up at the crack of dawn because Greenhill was so far away from my home. Martha drove me to the school, and by nine-thirty the test was over. I wasn't sure how I had done, but it really didn't matter because I wasn't too enthusiastic about going anyway. After the test, Wesley Kittleman, the admissions director, was to take me on a tour of the school. Greenhill was quite picturesque. There were lots of trees; the buildings looked new and much cleaner than my old school. I was particularly impressed with the gym and all the equipment. This, as I thought, was a perfect place to begin my professional career. It all looked great, but still I was mesmerized at how expensive it would be to go to a school like this. While walking down the corridor toward the cafeteria, Mr. Kittleman explained how the school would give me a scholarship and my mother wouldn't have to pay very much. My attitude began to change about this private school. It appeared to be the perfect place for my future and, besides, Mr. Kittleman, though he was white, wasn't stuck up afterall.

After about three weeks, I received a letter from Greenhill. I opened it and began to skim the words. I remember reading down to the words:

We're sorry, Mrs. Lemons. Your son's scores on our admissions test are not adequate for acceptance.

I immediately stopped reading. I sat back into my chair as if I were part of the décor. Nothing came from my mouth, but after a few seconds I could feel the tingle of water in my eyes. After a few minutes the drops turned to tears and began to run down my cheeks. I remember feeling as if I had deserved it. I thought I was so great and popular with all my friends, and now I was being punished for my self-indulgence. Then, of course, a period of self-pity rolled in. I felt that I was wronged, cheated and a victim of prejudice. I was shattered. I had been given the opportunity to better myself and, as I thought, it was all over.

Thanks to Greenhill, in the following summer I attended the Greenhill Summer Session and after careful consideration was admitted despite the fact that it would be a struggle. A struggle was an understatement. I had to change to a totally different environment of both social and economic backgrounds. Never had I been expected to do at least three to four hours of homework nightly and to be able to write five to ten page papers. I remember going through periods of saying "I can't," when I never really tried. However, with time and effort the transition began to occur. Some called it maturity, but I called it a new perspective on life. I have learned to interact and communicate with a diversity of people, no matter what race. I realize that if one asserts himself to his fullest potential then success in his own eyes can be reached. With the academic experience at Greenhill, no matter whether I play Pro basketball or not, I have the tools to shape my personal abilities in a positive manner toward the future. When asked the question—What experience has special meaning to me? It's simple and need not be stated.

"Seven years ago maybe I really said those things, but not anymore. Thanks, Martha."

There you have it. My essay presented here in *Expanding College Opportunity* is shown as it was written when I applied to college. I can see stylistic and word changes I might make if I were to rewrite my essay as an adult. But hey, that's okay. I, like most of you, was 17 years old when I applied to college. College admissions essays should reflect the style and voice of the student.

I encourage you to be blunt, to be courageous, to tell it like it is when it comes time for you to write your college admissions essay. Share what makes you unique and special. But whatever you choose to write about, I ask that you embrace the opportunity.

Discipline Report

You will most likely find a section on your college application that asks if you have had any "serious" discipline issues while in high school. (The Common Application and the Universal Application include a section on matters of discipline.)

Here's the deal: I hope you are not in a situation requiring you to complete the discipline section of a college application. I want to be direct and straightforward with you. It is not to your advantage to have a discipline record. And, you know what? Discipline issues, quite frankly, can be avoided. How? Be a respectful student to your teachers and your peers. Don't bully your peers. Obey the law. In short, you simply want to avoid the situation where you need to address discipline problems on your college applications.

Still, if you find yourself having to explain a discipline problem in your college application, I recommend that you be honest and up front about the situation. Be prepared to talk about the discipline situation and, more than anything else, be able to talk about what you learned from the situation. How have you grown as a person from having made a bad choice? How did you or will you move forward in the future?

You can take comfort in knowing that college admissions officers recognize that students (and, for that matter, all people) make mistakes. No one is perfect. You can be successful in the college admissions process even if you've had some type of serious discipline infraction. But, if you can avoid having a record of discipline problems, the college admissions process will be much smoother for you.

case study - terry

Terry was on the "A" honor roll for the past three semesters of his sophomore and junior year in high school. His parents were rightfully proud of him. Terry wanted to attend a college in a warm climate. His first and second choices for college were both located in Los Angeles, California.

During the summer between Terry's junior and senior year of high school, he met a kid, Joseph, in his neighborhood. Joseph, as well as Joseph's friends, had a reputation for being "bad boys." They were routinely getting in trouble with the police. Somehow, Terry got mixed up with Joseph and Joseph's buddies. Terry not only started to use illegal drugs, but he also started to sell drugs. One thing led to another and, in a matter of four to five months, Terry got arrested in a drug bust. During Terry's court hearing, he was sentenced to a

15-year prison term with a mandatory 10 years to serve. Sadly, Terry's dreams of going out West to college were shattered.

thoughts

Terry made some bad choices. He started to hang out with the wrong crowd and got involved with illegal drugs. Terry wasn't mature enough or lacked the support he needed to manage the negative peer influences. Regardless, Terry is responsible for his actions. Terry's poor choices landed him in jail, not college.

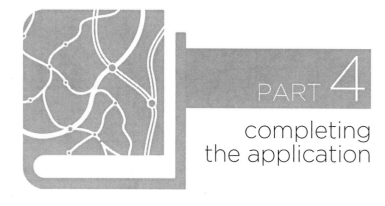

PART 4

completing
the application

Primary Audience:
Students

CHAPTER 7

when, where, and how to submit your college application

Now that we've covered in chapters five and six the elements that comprise your application to college, I turn to the mechanics of the admissions process. I start with the question: When should you submit your college admissions application?

There are a number of application submission deadlines. The date for you to submit your application can be different for each college. Therefore, you need to know the application submission dates that apply to the school(s) to which you want to apply. The quickest and easiest way to find out when you need to submit your application is to look at a college's website. You will most likely find application deadline information on the website's admissions and financial aid page. I strongly suggest you create a chart or timeline with the application deadlines, and include in your chart a plan for when you will complete each part of the application.

Submission deadlines include: Early Action, Early Decision, Regular Decision, and Rolling Admissions. Additionally, there are a few variations on some of the deadlines, such as Early Action I and Early Action II. While I will provide you with an explanation of the application deadlines, it is essential that you look at a college's website to learn the deadlines at a particular school. Again, I advise you to keep a written log of the date or time frame that your application(s) need to be submitted.

To illustrate how application deadlines work, let's assume you are a high school senior.

Regular Decision

If you apply Regular Decision, your application will be due sometime in December or January of your senior year. You will most likely hear whether or not you have been admitted to a school in March or April. If you request financial aid, a college's financial aid officer(s) will provide you with a financial aid offer or award letter near the time (or a few weeks after) you receive an acceptance letter. Assuming you applied, as I've suggested, to a "basket" of schools, and if you are denied admission to a school(s), you will most likely have admission offers from other colleges.

Early Decision

If you apply Early Decision, you will submit your application to only one college sometime in the early fall, typically in the October or November time frame. You will receive notification about your Early Decision acceptance or denial by mid December. If you are accepted to the college, your Early Decision application commits you to attend that particular college. In this regard, your Early Decision application is therefore binding. You will learn about your financial aid package shortly after you are accepted. If there is a legitimate reason that your Early Decision financial aid offer is inadequate, this might be the one way you can be excused or released from a binding Early Decision agreement. You would need to talk with the school officials where you were accepted about your situation. The good news about being accepted to a college via an Early Decision submittal is that the application process is, for the most part, complete. You can move forward with enjoying the remaining months of your senior year. Of course, you want to continue to perform well in your classes.

If you are not accepted Early Decision, then a college may do one of two things:

1) *place you on their wait-list*

   By being placed on a wait-list, a college is letting you know that you will be notified of their final decision on your application in the spring (March or April)—the same time the school notifies applicants who applied Regular Decision. (Remember, the Early Decision pool is much smaller than the Regular Decision pool.) If you are placed on the wait-list, you must apply to other schools.

2) *deny your admission*

   If you are denied admission during the Early Decision review, I suggest that you simply move forward with applying to other colleges. There is no need to get down on yourself. There is a school for you. Do note: you will almost immediately have to submit applications to other colleges. For that reason, I recommend that you continue to work on preparing applications to other colleges even while you wait to hear the results of your Early Decision application.

Early Action

Early Action is a blend between Regular Decision and Early Decision. You submit your application early—in October or November. A college's admissions officers will let you know if you are accepted in the fall, probably around mid-December. If you are admitted, you benefit by knowing—early—that you have the option of attending that particular school. The Early Action offer is non-binding, meaning you have the option to apply to other colleges. There is also Early Action I and Early Action II, which operate like Early Action with the exception that the specific submission dates and notification dates of the admission decision are different.

Rolling Admissions

If a college utilizes a Rolling Admissions application cycle, there is not a predefined submission date. Generally speaking, you decide when you want to apply, though I typically recommend students apply as early as possible, as there are a limited number of applicants who will be admitted. (A school may have some parameters on when you can submit your application.) After you submit your application, you could receive an answer as early as two to three weeks after applying.

Which application submission date should you follow?

It's up to you.

- If you are committed to attending a particular college, then applying Early Decision is a good option. Keep in mind that you absolutely must communicate with your school counselors and recommenders in the early fall (August or early September) about your desire to apply Early Decision so that these individuals can begin preparing the necessary forms on your behalf.

- If you want your first semester senior year grades to be reviewed by an admissions committee in hopes that the grades will improve your candidacy for admission, then Regular Decision or Rolling Admissions is a good option. Your first semester senior year grades and community involvement will not be considered if you apply Early Decision.

- If you want to consider a number of schools, along with their respective financial aid award offers, then applying Regular Decision might be the better option.

Which form(s) or application(s) do you need in order to apply to a college?

Colleges produce admissions applications that you can use for their school. In this case, you would complete an application for each school to which you want to apply.

Today, an increasingly popular way to apply to college is by completing the Common Application. The Common Application is a standard form that can be submitted to as many schools as you want. You must pay for each submission and only some colleges are on the Common Application list of members. The advantage of using the Common Application is that you only have to complete one application form. The Common Application saves you time. You can focus on one application, though some colleges that accept the Common Application require supplemental short essays that are only applicable to that particular school.

To find out which colleges utilize the Common Application and to access the Common Application, visit www.commonapp.org. Similar to the Common Application is the Universal Application. You fill out one application and choose among a list of member schools. Information about the Universal Application can be downloaded at www.universalcollegeapp.com.

Finally, I want to make special mention of the fact that there are a number of national and local, not-for-profit and community-based organizations that have formed partnerships or associations with colleges in order to increase the number of highly qualified low-income students who pursue higher education. The Posse Foundation (www.possefoundation.org), Questbridge (www.questbridge.org), and Project GRAD Atlanta (www.atlanta.projectgrad.org) are examples of such organizations.

Questbridge, for example, provides a single application (similar to the Common Application) that may be used at a number of highly selective colleges, such as Emory University, Dartmouth College, Oberlin College, Princeton University, and Vanderbilt University. Plus, Questbridge provides access to fully paid scholarships to its partner schools.

To find the names of other organizations that aim to help students go to college, I recommend you visit the National College Access Network website, www.collegeaccess.org.

Where do you get a college application?

Here are three common ways to obtain an application or submit your information to a college:

- Download an admissions application from a college's website.
- Input your information into a college's online application.
- Phone or email a college's admissions office and request an application.

How should you submit your college application?

Typically, colleges will give you several options to submit your application.

- If you submit your application through the mail, make sure you send it with enough time to meet the application deadline.
- If you apply online, make sure your application is completed and submitted at least two to three days before the deadline.

You absolutely do not want to wait until the last minute to submit your online application. Why? You could run into technical or computer problems with submitting your application. You want to leave yourself with enough time to be able to submit your application via regular mail or overnight mail in case of an emergency.

How much does it cost to apply to college?

Application fees range from approximately $35 to $100.

What if you cannot afford an application fee?

- Look on the admissions page of a college's website for information on obtaining an application fee waiver. There are eligibility guidelines for fee waivers posted on a college's website.
- Talk to your high school counselor about obtaining an application fee waiver.
- Both the College Board and the ACT are also resources where you can obtain college application fee waivers. View www.collegeboard.org or www.act.org.
- Just as the cost or sticker price of a college should not stop you from applying, you should definitely not let an application fee stop you from applying to college. If you cannot afford to pay an application fee, call or email an admissions representative at the college to which you want to apply and explain your financial situation. Admissions representatives want to help students. Be at ease with reaching out for help.

How many schools should you apply to?

There is no set number. Students commonly apply to 5 to 10 colleges. I recommend that, at a minimum, you apply to at least 3 to 5 colleges. Because of the internet and the popularity of the Common Application, a number of students apply to as many as 15 to 20 colleges. The number of schools to which you apply is a personal decision. But remember: you will only attend one school; it costs money to apply to schools (there is a limit on the number of application fee waivers you can get); and it takes time to apply to college. So then, it behooves you to give careful thought about where you choose to apply.

CHAPTER 8

deciding on which college to enroll

You have thought about what's important to you in choosing a college. You've identified a "basket" of schools to apply to. The work of completing applications is behind you. Now what? The next major component of the admissions process is waiting on an admissions notice of acceptance or denial in the mail (or via a school's website). What to do with a college's notice of acceptance or denial is the focus of this chapter. Let's start with a denial notification, and then move on to the coveted acceptance letter and the decision of which college to enroll.

Denial Notifications

If you receive a denial of admission notification, it may be natural for you to feel some disappointment. Don't take a denial letter too personally. Being denied admission is often more an issue of numbers—a larger number of applicants to a school relative to a smaller number of available places for an incoming class. Additionally, a school may have a high priority to recruit a student with a specific academic or extracurricular background versus another student.

Simply stated: I would not recommend that you waste time trying to figure out the rationale behind a school's admissions decision. The decision of an admissions committee is complex. Their decision centers on all the factors that I have covered in *Expanding College Opportunity*. With so many students applying to colleges, the very nature of the admissions process is one that is often driven by admissions officers having to parse through a crowded pool of talented and equally deserving applicants. Depending on the type of college and the current recruitment goals of that college, the priorities of who should be admitted can vary from year to year. Likewise, college admissions decisions can be based on very subtle, subjective differences between candidates.

Acceptance Letters

If you receive an offer of admission from one or more colleges, then first I want to congratulate you. Secondly, you must now decide where you want to enroll. Herein is where you should begin to carefully evaluate the admissions and financial aid award letters you receive. You want to be crystal clear about what is being offered to you, particularly as it relates to financial aid. Is your offer of admission contingent on any requirements? If you are admitted with an offer of an academic scholarship, do you have to maintain a certain grade point average (GPA) in order to continue receiving your scholarship? If, for example, you are a student-athlete who is admitted with an offer of an athletic scholarship, you need to know the college's policies regarding your role as both an athlete and a student. If you are injured and cannot play your sport, then what happens? Is the athletic scholarship applicable only for the first year of college? Or, is the scholarship "guaranteed" for all four (or five or six years) of college? Bottom line: if you have any questions about your offer of admission or your scholarship offer, get answers. Contact a school's admissions or financial aid office and ask your questions.

If you are deciding between more than one school, I encourage you to review your earlier notes about the colleges (hopefully you kept them). You may not follow your notes to the letter. Your feelings about a school may have changed from the time you started researching colleges to the time you receive an offer of admission. However, your notes can be helpful in reminding you of important considerations that you might want to keep in mind as you now decide where to enroll.

If possible, you may also want to visit or revisit a school before you make your final decision. Having the opportunity to spend time, or more time, on a campus can give you a greater feel for the school and aid you in making a decision. Believe it or not, some colleges will even pay for (or significantly contribute towards) the cost of visiting their school after you've been admitted. This offer is usually extended to admitted students who may not be able to afford to visit a college before they make their final decision on where to attend. If you are admitted to a college, don't be afraid to ask if a college offers such a college-sponsored visit program, particularly if you feel like you would otherwise not be able to visit a school that you are seriously considering.

What to do after you make your decision on where to enroll?

- After you decide where you want to enroll, notify the college that you accept their offer of admission. In an offer of admission, the college will usually explain their procedures on how to notify them of your desire to enroll.

- Let the other schools where you were accepted know that you will not enroll. This will enable them to offer your spot to another student.

- Finally, let the people that helped you with the admissions process hear your good news. Call them. Write them. Thank them. And, by the way, I would be especially pleased if you told other families that my book played an important role in helping you in the admissions process. Just sayin'.

case study - jeff & cheryl

Jeff had a 4.0 GPA and took 4 AP classes as a senior in high school. He was editor of the student newspaper, and earned a varsity letter on the lacrosse team during all four years of high school. Cheryl, on the other hand, had a 3.5 GPA and, for the most part, took standard-level classes in high school; Cheryl did, however, take AP calculus and honors French IV as a senior. Unlike Jeff, Cheryl was not as active in high school because she worked part-time as a waitress two days during the week and on the weekends. Cheryl needed the money to help her family and to pay for school expenses. For example, Cheryl bought her own school clothes and supplies, as well as the school necessities of her two younger brothers. As luck would have it, both Jeff and Cheryl applied to the same prestigious college in Nashville, Tennessee. Guess who got in?

Jeff and Cheryl were both admitted.

thoughts

The admissions committee sought to understand Jeff and Cheryl's individual stories, and to assess how they might uniquely contribute to the college community. Cheryl, in particular, did an outstanding job of telling her story in the college admissions essays. The admissions officers were able to clearly understand Cheryl's background from her essays. Cheryl's college admissions essays played a key role in the admissions process.

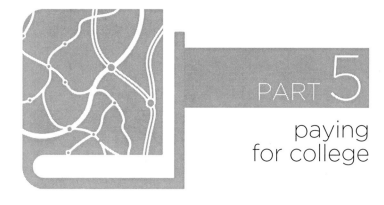

PART 5

paying
for college

Primary Audience:
Parents and Students

CHAPTER 9

the financial aid process: making it work for you

Students and parents are sometimes intimidated by the cost of attending college. For that reason, students may not apply to a particular school, or a student may not apply to any college. So here is my overall message to you (students) regarding college finances: **do not let the cost of a college stop you from applying.** Depending on the school that you are considering, you may pay little to no money to attend. A good number of colleges, especially well endowed or financed private colleges, have a need-blind admission policy in which case a school will consider your application for admission without regard to your ability to pay.

To make the college financial aid process work for you, it is important that you understand the basics of the financial aid equation. I put the equation into three boxes and explain the contents of each box separately.

Exhibit 3

BOX 3	BOX 2	BOX 1
Tuition or Sticker Price and Cost of Attendance	Expected Family Contribution (EFC)	Demonstrated Financial Need

BOX 3

Tuition and Cost of Attendance

Box 3 includes both a college's tuition or sticker price and its cost of attendance. Admissions and financial aid officers may also refer collectively to both items in Box 3 as the Cost of Attendance, in which case admissions officers lump both the tuition and other attendance expenses together.

Tuition

The tuition or sticker price is the price that you often see listed on websites and literature about a school.

Cost of Attendance

Cost of attendance includes the following expenses:

- Books and supplies

- Student Fees
- Transportation to and from college
- Food
- Housing
- Miscellaneous living expenses

All together, Box 3 is an estimate of the total amount of money a student will need to attend a given college.

BOX 2
Expected Family Contribution (EFC)

The Expected Family Contribution is a federal government calculation or formula that is used to help a college determine the amount of money you or your family will be expected to pay towards the Cost of Attendance (Box 3). The Expected Family Contribution is a figure that is derived from information you provide on the FAFSA (Free Application for Federal Student Aid).

What is the FAFSA? The FAFSA (www.fafsa.gov) is a form published by the Federal Government. The FAFSA is used to calculate your Expected Family Contribution and ultimately it is used to determine your financial need. The FAFSA is FREE. The FAFSA takes about 30-45 minutes to complete and should be submitted to the U.S. Department of Education (online or at the address indicated on the FAFSA form) at the earliest possible date after January 1st of your senior year. The FAFSA enables you to receive financial aid. I want to be especially clear here. The FAFSA is the single most important form you need to complete in order to get money to pay for college. Completing the FAFSA is a must do.

Some colleges will ask you to complete a form called a College Scholarship Service PROFILE (CSS PROFILE), which is a financial aid form that is similar to the FAFSA. A financial aid officer will consider data from the FAFSA or the CSS PROFILE or both in order to determine the amount and type of financial aid for which you are eligible.

BOX 1

If you subtract the Expected Family Contribution (Box 2) from the total Cost of Attendance (Box 3) then you will arrive at a calculation of your financial gap or Demonstrated Financial Need. The Demonstrated Financial Need can be satisfied by some combination of the following four components:

1. Grants: Money that a college gives you or allots on your behalf in order to pay for your tuition and the cost of attendance (Box 3). The great thing about Grants is that you do not have to pay the money back.

2. Scholarships: Similar to Grant funds, you do not have to pay scholarship money back. There are two general categories of scholarships:

- Institutional Scholarships—money that a college awards you based on your academic record, "special talent", athletic ability, or some other personal attribute.

- Outside Scholarships—money that you receive from outside public and private organizations that provide scholarship funds to students. As far as the outside organizations are concerned, students are often required to submit scholarship applications to obtain the funds. The scholarship applications are similar to college applications in that you complete forms, write essays, and submit an application in accordance with specific deadlines. Two examples of well-known outside scholarships are the National Merit Scholarship (www.nationalmerit.org) and the Gates Millennium Scholars Program (www.gmsp.org).

Sometimes you will hear admissions and financial aid officers talk about the "net price" to attend a college. What they are referring to is the amount of money you will actually pay to attend a college from your family's funds and the student loans you might incur.

3. Work-study: A program that assists you with securing an on campus part-time job at a college in which case you may work eight to 10 hours a week in order to help you pay for your daily expenses while at college.

4. Loans: Money you receive in the form of a loan in order to pay for college. In the case of Federal loans, you do not have to begin paying the money back until after you leave or graduate from college. Types of loans include:

- Federal Perkins Loans
- Subsidized Federal Stafford Loans
- Unsubsidized Federal Stafford Loans
- Federal Plus Loans for Parents (based on the parent's credit score)
- Private Loans

case study - anna

When Ana immigrated from Spain to Washington D.C., her English language skills were just so, so. Ana took English as a Second Language Classes (ESL) at a local church in order to improve her ability to communicate. As her English language skills improved, Ana enrolled in a community college. She took for-credit classes that were not language intensive, such as math and art. She eventually got her associate degree. Ana then transferred to a four-year public university and later earned a bachelor's of science degree in microelectronic engineering. She is now preparing to go back to school to get a master's degree in business administration (M.B.A.).

thoughts

Ana's story is impressive. For most people in Ana's situation, the idea of going to a U.S. college would seem unattainable. But not for Ana. Ana did not let her language skills stop her from going to college. Ana had a plan, and she worked that plan. Ana has the potential to earn over $100,000 a year after she completes her M.B.A. And, she will be able to send money back home to Spain in order to help her extended family. Ana's college education has been a true stepping-stone for Ana and her family. Felicidades, Ana!

Financial Strategies

Now that I've covered the basics of financial aid and specifically the financial aid equation, let's talk strategy. In order to prepare for the investment you will make in getting your college degree, I share key steps to paying for college:

- Starting from today, I encourage parents and students to save as much money as possible for future college costs. The amount is up to you. Ten dollars each month, fifty dollars each month, two hundred dollars each month. Save whatever amount you can realistically afford.

- Consider saving via a college savings plan. Here's one scenario to illustrate the benefit of investing in a college savings plan:
  o A family saves $100 each month from the time a student starts 8th grade to the time he or she starts college 5 years later.
  o The college savings fund yields a 7% annual rate of return.
  o A student will have an estimated $7,201 by the time he or she is ready to enter college.
  o If a family saves more money each month and starts to save when the student is younger, let's say in elementary school, the total saved for college will be exponentially more.

I know from personal experience that it's not always easy to save money, let alone to save for college. But, if families can save as much as possible, beginning early in a student's life, then the power of compounding interest will work to give you a financial base to start college.

• Make sure your list of prospective schools ranges in Cost of Attendance (referring to Box 3 of the financial aid equation).

• Most, if not all colleges, ask if you intend to apply for financial aid. Answer "yes."

• Complete the FAFSA (www.fafsa.gov) and, if required, the CSS PROFILE (www.collegeboard.org). The FAFSA and the CSS PROFILE are the gateway to getting financial aid.

• Know that most students who attend college do not pay the full-price or sticker price listed on websites. At private colleges in particular, I estimate that less than 30% of students (perhaps I should say their families) actually pay the full price. For this reason, there is no reason for any student to feel any sense of shame, stigma, or embarrassment about applying for financial aid. I remember applying for financial aid when I was completing applications for college. And let me tell you…I am happy the aid was available.

• Talk with admissions and financial aid representatives and ask about their approach and polices concerning financial aid. Many private colleges are able to pay the full Demonstrated Financial Need of students. For instance, if you apply and are admitted to a college that costs $60,000 per year, but you or your family can only afford to pay $5,000 per year, the college may cover the $55,000 difference in cost. You should never assume you can't go to a particular college just because you see a high sticker price on a website.

• Throughout high school, research and apply for outside scholarships (Box 1) sponsored by companies, foundations, community organizations, and state agencies. One of the easiest ways to obtain a scholarship is to perform well in your high school classes and to participate in some type of community service or extracurricular activity. I am also compelled to say that I know of plenty of students who think that they can just be a good athlete and win a scholarship to college. That's a nice idea. It can happen. But, the reality of the situation is that only 1-2% of students receive athletic scholarships to college, as reported on the www.finaid.org website created by Mark Kantrowitz. Thus, I encourage students to think of themselves as scholars and focus on doing their best work in school in order to get SCHOLARship money.

• If you utilize scholarship databases, you can find scholarship opportunities based on your academic and personal background. Here again, I hope students will understand that doing well in classes can lead to being awarded more money to pay for college. And, you don't have to have perfect grades to get a scholarship. Good grades help (a lot), but there are all types of scholarships available. Here are key scholarship and general financial aid database websites:

o https://bigfuture.collegeboard.org/scholarship-search

o www.fastweb.com

o www.finaid.org

o www.nasfaa.org

o www.savingforcollege.com

o www.scholarships.com

• It is important that you follow a school's financial aid guidelines and deadlines. If you miss a deadline, there may be fewer or no funds available for you. (A school may have a Rolling Admissions policy: but if you need financial aid, I suggest you apply sooner rather than later.)

• Be open and frank in your communication with a school's admissions and financial aid staff. This is not the time to be shy. Everybody's financial situation is different. Communicate your family situation and what financial resources you feel you need to enroll in a school.

• If you want more information about the financial aid process beyond what I cover in *Expanding College Opportunity*, I recommend you view www.studentaid.gov and go on YouTube and type in Federal Student Aid (www.youtube.com/ federalstudentaid). The website and the Federal Student Aid videos on YouTube are awesome. The information is provided by the Federal Government and is presented in a way that is clear and straightforward. You can also call the Federal Student Aid office at 1-800-433-3243. Of course, there are other websites that provide detailed information about financial aid and scholarships, such as http://knowhow2go.acenet.edu and www.fafsa.gov, but I think the Federal Student Aid website and the Federal Student Aid office should be at the top of your list of available information resources.

- More than anything else, it is important that you embrace the belief that you can go to college. Sometimes you have to be your own best advocate. Ask questions. Get answers. Work to get the results you want.

Exhibit 4

The Financial Aid Equation: 3-2=1

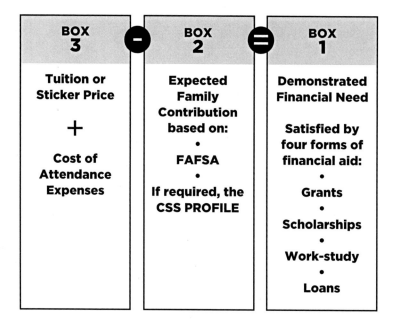

BOX 3	−	BOX 2	=	BOX 1
Tuition or Sticker Price + Cost of Attendance Expenses		Expected Family Contribution based on: • FAFSA • If required, the CSS PROFILE		Demonstrated Financial Need Satisfied by four forms of financial aid: • Grants • Scholarships • Work-study • Loans

Key Strategies

Box 3:

- Apply to a range or "basket" of schools.

- Don't be afraid to apply to schools with high sticker prices. Some schools may offer you a full-scholarship based on your Demonstrated Financial Need (Box 1).

- Make sure you save for college and do a thorough job of understanding and budgeting for the cost of attendance.

Box 2:

- Complete the FAFSA. It doesn't matter if you believe your family is too rich or too poor to get financial aid. Complete the FAFSA. Completing the FAFSA creates an opportunity for college applicants to receive federal financial aid.

- Complete the CSS PROFILE if the college(s) you are applying to require the form.

- Make sure you submit the FAFSA at the earliest possible date possible after January 1st of your senior year. You will need to complete the FAFSA for each year of college. If you have any difficulty with completing the form, call the FAFSA office at 1-800-433-3243.

Box 1:

- Colleges determine your financial aid award based on the Student Aid Report (SAR) that is generated as a result of your completing the FAFSA. After you complete the FAFSA, you will receive the SAR. Check your SAR and make sure it is accurate. If it is not, contact the Federal Student Aid office immediately in order to correct the information. It's always helpful if you can get more grants and scholarships, as opposed to loans. You don't have to pay grant and scholarship money back.

- Consider loans as an investment in your future, but try to only borrow as much as you think you need. You'll eventually have to pay the loan money back.

- To better understand the types of loans (e.g. Federal Perkins Loans, Subsidized Loans, Unsubsidized Loans, etc.), view the www.studentaid.gov website. Before you take out a loan make sure you understand the type of loan and the stipulations that go with it. The studentaid.gov website does a great job of outlining the features of each type of loan.

case study - sheila

Sheila had a 3.85 GPA, ran on the varsity track team, and sang in her church choir. Every summer during high school, she worked at a sandwich shop near Euclid and Laclede in the Central West End in St. Louis. Sheila's father raised her because her mom died of breast cancer when Sheila was five years old. By all accounts, Sheila was a hard worker and a solid student. Sheila could have gone to almost any college she wanted to. Unfortunately, she didn't. Shelia chose not to apply to college. She was worried that her dad couldn't afford to pay for school. Shelia already felt guilty because her father had sacrificed so much for her. Today, Sheila continues to work at the sandwich shop.

thoughts

Sheila had options. The biggest issue for Sheila was her concern about paying for college. Sheila could have enrolled in a community college, technical or trade school, or some other type of accredited college program. But, more than anything else, Sheila needed to complete the FAFSA. She probably would have gotten a "full ride" (scholarship) to attend college. Shelia clearly hurt her opportunity to attend college by not completing the FAFSA and taking the necessary steps to apply for financial aid.

PART 6

a roadmap
for success

**Primary Audience:
Parents and Students**

CHAPTER 10

five principles
to ensure academic success

I've participated in a number of academic and executive education programs, as well as continuing education courses. These degree and non-degree opportunities enabled me to attend a number of colleges and universities. The list includes Amherst College, Emory University, Georgetown University, George Washington University, Harvard University, Northwestern University, The University of California at Los Angeles (UCLA), and several community colleges.

Based on my experience, I have learned a lot about "how to learn" and ultimately how to perform well in academic environments. I don't think there is a single answer or perfect approach to doing well in school. But, I have found that there are some key principles that serve as the foundation of success in school, and for that matter, in professional environments. I share these five principles with you.

Principle #1. Have a sense of purpose about your studies and your life

Students need to feel a sense of purpose. A sense of purpose or vision gives you a direction and target to aim for. Further, a sense of purpose will help to motivate you to do well in high school, college and your life after college. Self-motivation is at the foundation of my principle number two.

Principle #2. Be self-motivated

What does a self-motivated student look like and act like? Here are some behaviors:

- Completes school assignments before the deadline
- Stays focused in classes
- Listens intently to teachers and peers
- Asks questions in class
- Seeks to improve in his or her studies
- Reads extra or outside material related to class assignments in an effort to master the subject, as well as to gain a different perspective on the material
- Asks for help

Principle #3. Become highly organized

Practice being organized. Create to-do lists. Plan your activities. The more you organize yourself the better you will do. Organization works.

Here is an organization to-do list:

- Work Space—organize your work space, i.e. desk, room, closet, etc.
- Develop a storage or shelving space for your books. Keep all your books and supplies in their proper place.

- Create a system where your school papers/assignments go into folders. Label the sections.

- Keep track of current and upcoming assignments by recording your assignments in a calendar or planner. Don't rely on your memory to record assignments and upcoming tests. Write assignment due dates on a calendar. Then work backward from the due date, creating/identifying dates for goals to accomplish in order to complete the assignment on time.

- When you are assigned papers and projects, organize yourself so that you can start studying or preparing an assignment far in advance of the due date. Prep time enables you to be better prepared and to do a better job on an assignment.

I speak from personal experience when I say that effective organization and study skills are fundamental to doing well in high school and in college.

Principle #4. Be open and willing to get support

- People need people. Reach out to other people when you need help. Be willing to collaborate.

- If you have an advisor at school, go to that person for advice about school. Talk to your advisor if things are going well, or if you are having difficulty. If you do not have an advisor, get one. Ask a teacher for help with getting an advisor or guidance counselor.

- Get a tutor. Don't be ashamed about having a tutor. Tutoring is a good thing. Students who perform well in high school often have tutors. Tutoring may come in the form of private tutoring or group-tutoring. By having a tutor, you will have someone to help ensure you understand class material.

- Go to your teacher's office hours. Sometimes students are intimidated or shy about going to a teacher's office hours. Big mistake. Talking with a teacher during his or her office hours or at an appointed time can be incredibly helpful. In a one-to-one situation, your teacher may explain a topic that you are having difficulty with in a way that is much more comprehensible than in a class setting.

Principle #5. Develop your core academic skills in reading, writing, and mathematics

High school teachers and college professors aim to develop your problem-solving and critical thinking skills. By problem-solving and critical thinking, I mean your ability to analyze problems and develop solutions. Additionally, teachers seek to nurture your creativity so that you can pose new questions or formulate new ideas. Three academic areas support your creativity and critical thinking skills. Continually work to develop these three skills or subject areas:

1) Reading

Reading is a crucial, life-long skill. In all your high school and college classes, you will have to read in order to do well.

Develop a practice of reading. One of the easiest ways to do this is to read subjects you naturally enjoy. (Of course, you must do the reading assigned to you in school.) Read at least 20 to 30 minutes of unassigned reading each day.

Earlier in the book, I talked about the benefits of reading to improve your scores on standardized tests. I want to reiterate my point: having strong reading skills will improve your grades in school and raise your scores on the ACT, SAT, and the SAT Subject Tests.

2) Writing

Writing is a core skill. Your ability to communicate well in writing will improve your grades in high school and college. Writing is also important even if you plan to pursue a college major or professional career in a science, technology, engineering, or math field (STEM). Regardless of your chosen profession, you cannot escape the need to be able to communicate effectively verbally and in writing.

It is sometimes hard for a student to know if he or she is a strong writer. My advice is to practice writing. Get feedback on your writing. The feedback may come from a teacher at school or through a private writing workshop. TheSecretToWriting.com is a resource to improve your writing skills.

3) Math

Quantitative skills help you in a number of courses, particularly in math and science related classes.

Unlike writing classes, it is easier to tell whether your math skills are strong or not. The answer to a math question is either correct or incorrect. Consequently, you have an objective way to determine if you need help in mathematics.

I know that I've presented the five principles in a direct, matter of fact, kinda way. The principles work. Follow these five principles and you will get into and graduate from college … on time. The principles have worked for me in academic settings, as well as in professional environments.

CHAPTER 11

staying on track from middle school through high school

In chapter 11, I provide key action items for students and parents to stay on track during each year of middle school and high school. I suggest you read the bullet points for each grade level carefully because I make subtle and not so subtle recommendations for each academic year.

8th Grade

Students

- Focus on school in order to start high school on a positive note. You may be able to take more advanced classes during your first year of high school, such as Honors Algebra, Geometry, or an advanced literature class.
- Take a writing class before high school. You will be expected to write well in high school and certainly once you are in college.
- The summer before the start of high school read a book on "how to study." Strong study skills will make a tremendous difference in your academic success during high school.
- Organize your work space at home.
- Identify tutors in your community that can help you with your core courses in high school, i.e. math, science, English,

and social studies. College admissions officers will devote special attention to how you perform in these core classes.

- Begin thinking about the courses you will enroll in during high school, from your first year of high school through your senior year. Some first-year and sophomore year classes are prerequisites for upper level high school classes. Think about the sequence of courses you may take.
- If you use social media websites, make sure you do not have offensive material on your social media pages.
- Have lots of fun during the summer before 9th grade. You want to be prepared to start high school with a sense of purpose and an attitude that reflects a desire to perform at your best.

Parents

- Save money for your child's college education.
- Work to make sure you have a good credit score in case you decide you want to apply for a Federal Plus Loan or a private loan for your student.
- Stay abreast of your child's daily or weekly assignments and grades. But, don't obsess about the grades.
- Visit your child's school and make sure you meet your son or daughter's teachers. Attend every parent-teacher conference.
- During the summer before 9th grade, have a conversation with your child about the expectations of a high school student. Specifically, it is important that students understand that it is their responsibility to complete all assignments

in high school, to study for tests and quizzes, to write and carefully edit all papers, and to turn in assignments on time. These requirements are not the responsibility of the parent. If you, as a parent, can help your student recognize and embrace the responsibility of managing his or her educational success, then both parents and the student will find the high school years to be more enjoyable and certainly less stressful.

9th Grade

Students

Grades & Course Selection

- Be a good student.
- Complete and submit all class assignments on time.
- Follow a college prep program. Assuming you take seven courses each year, in 9th grade you might take:
  1. English
  2. Math
  3. Science
  4. Foreign or "World" Language
  5. History
  6. Elective course
  7. Elective course

Standardized Tests

- Read, read, read.
- Review practice tests and focus on the reading and writing section.
- Take advantage of any available FREE prep courses.

Extracurricular Activities

- Be involved in activities and programs outside of school such as community service.
- If you use social media websites, be sure you do not have offensive material on your social media pages.

Parents

- Save money for your child's college education.
- Work to make sure you have a good credit score in case you decide you want to apply for a Federal Plus Loan or a private loan for your student.
- Stay abreast of your child's daily or weekly assignments and grades. But, don't obsess on the grades.
- Visit your child's school and make sure you meet your son or daughter's teachers.
- Assist your son or daughter with identifying tutors for core academic classes or classes in which your student may have difficulty.

10th

Students

Grades & Course Selection

- Be a good student.
- Complete and submit all class assignments on time.
- Follow a college prep program. Assuming you take seven courses each year, in 10th grade you might take:
  1. English

2. Math

3. Science

4. Foreign or "World" Language

5. Social Science

6. Elective course

7. Elective course

Standardized Tests

- Read, read, read.
- Start reviewing for all sections (reading, writing, and math) of the SAT or ACT. Utilize exercise books and FREE practice exercises on the College Board and ACT websites.
- Take advantage of any available FREE prep courses.

Extracurricular Activities

- Be involved in activities and programs outside of school such as community service.
- If you did not enjoy your extracurricular activities in 9th grade, then try a new activity.
- If you use social media websites, be sure you do not have offensive material on your social media pages.

Summer Break

- Do some standardized test practice during the summer.
- Consider taking a SAT Subject Test, if appropriate.
- Participate in some type of volunteer service, internship, or academic enrichment program.

- Have fun during your summer break and be prepared to work especially hard during your junior and senior years.

Parents

- Save money for your child's college education.
- Work to make sure you have a good credit score in case you decide you want to apply for a Federal Plus Loan or a private loan for your student.
- Attend college admissions and college financial aid information sessions at your son or daughter's high school or in your community.
- Stay abreast of your child's daily or weekly assignments and grades. But, don't obsess on the grades.
- Visit your child's school and make sure you meet your son or daughter's teachers.
- Assist your son or daughter with identifying tutors for core academic classes or classes in which your student may have difficulty.

11th

Students

Grades & Course Selection

- It is important to do well in your classes. Make it happen.
- Complete and submit all class assignments on time.
- If you are planning to apply Early Decision to a college, the grades you earn during your junior year are the last set of

grades college admissions officers will see before making their admissions decision.

- Meet with your high school counselor about college options.
- Follow a college prep program. Assuming you take seven courses each year, in 11th grade you might take:
  1. English
  2. Math
  3. Science
  4. Foreign or "World" Language
  5. Social Science
  6. Elective course
  7. Elective course

Standardized Tests

- Take the PSAT or PLAN at your high school in the fall.
- Take the SAT in the Spring (May or June).
- Take SAT Subject Tests in the Spring.
- Take advantage of any available FREE prep courses.

Extracurricular Activities

- Continue with at least one or two activities that you participated in during 9th and 10th grade. Try to assume a leadership role. Immerse yourself. Enjoy yourself.
- If you use social media websites, be sure you do not have offensive material on your social media pages.

Recommendations
- Ask teachers for college recommendations before your summer break.

Spring and Summer Breaks
- Develop a prospective list or "basket" of schools to apply to.
- Visit colleges.
- Work on your college admissions essays during the summer between junior and senior year.
- Research scholarship opportunities. Identify key scholarships that you want to apply to by exploring scholarships databases (listed in the paying for college section of *Expanding College Opportunity*). Start the scholarship application process.

Parents
- Save money for your child's college education.
- Work to make sure you have a good credit score in case you decide you want to apply for a Federal Plus Loan or a private loan for your student.
- Attend college admissions and college financial aid information sessions at your son or daughter's high school.
- Stay abreast of your child's daily or weekly assignments and grades. But, don't obsess on the grades.
- Visit your child's school and make sure you meet your son or daughter's teachers.
- Assist your son or daughter with identifying tutors for core academic classes or classes in which your student may have difficulty.

Students

Grades & Course Selection

- First semester grades are especially important. Perform at your best. But remember, you need to do well throughout your entire senior year. Don't slack off. Colleges can easily withdraw an offer of admission if your grades "significantly" decline.

- Complete and submit all class assignments on time.

- If you use social media websites, be sure you do not have offensive material on your social media pages.

- Follow a college prep program. Assuming you take seven courses each year, in 12th grade you might take:

  1. English
  2. Math
  3. Science
  4. Foreign or "World" Language
  5. Social Science
  6. Elective course
  7. Elective course

Standardized Tests

- Re-take the SAT or ACT if you aim to earn a higher score.
- Take SAT Subject Tests, if appropriate.

College Applications

- Apply to a "basket" of colleges.

- Complete the FAFSA as soon as possible after January 1st.
- Pay attention to admissions and financial aid deadlines.
- Maintain ongoing communication with your high school counselor.
- Carefully review your offers of admission and financial aid packages.

Summer Break
- Enjoy your summer break before the start of college.
- Make sure you follow the enrollment guidelines of the college where you plan to matriculate.
- Read a "how to study" book. Trust me. You'll need the study skills in college.
- Take a writing course. Writing is a skill that will largely impact your academic success during college.
- Congratulate yourself. You did it. You're on the road to college.

Parents
- Save money for your child's college education.
- Work to make sure you have a good credit score in case you decide you want to apply for a Federal Plus Loan or a private loan for your student.
- Stay abreast of your child's daily or weekly assignments and grades. But, don't obsess on the grades.
- Visit your child's school and make sure you meet your son or daughter's teachers.

- Assist your son or daughter with identifying tutors for core academic classes or classes in which your student may be having difficulty.

- Recognize that the college application process may be stressful for your child and you. If there are moments that your child appears overwhelmed, try to be supportive. Give your child the opportunity to take the lead in working through the college application process, and offer assistance to your child as is appropriate.

- Enjoy the time with your child before he or she starts college.

CONCLUSION
reflections on the journey

I close *Expanding College Opportunity* by talking directly to students and parents. I also speak briefly in regards to the specific admissions requirements of international students.

A note to students:

Pursue higher education. I often say to students: the opportunity to go to college is one of our greatest treasures. The college experience opens your eyes and mind to new ideas and self-discovery.

Set personal goals. I'm sure your parents, other family members, teachers, and friends will help you to be successful. But ultimately, I want you to remember that you have to take responsibility for your own actions and effort. Study. Do well in your classes. Get involved in your community. These are all things that are in your control. Other people can't do these things for you.

Know you have the power to succeed. Go for your dreams. With effort and determination you can go to college and graduate.

Make a commitment to give your best to school and in turn you will give your best to yourself. You deserve it. There is no getting around the fact that you have to work hard in order to do well in school and, for that matter, to do well in life. You be the judge as to whether or not you are giving a 100% effort in your studies or your involvement in community activities.

Be determined to succeed and don't let peer pressure steer you down the wrong path. When I was growing up, I, like many students, experienced peer pressure. For example:

- Peer pressure to do illegal activities
- Peer pressure to have sex as a teenager
- Peer pressure to use drugs

I'm here to tell you that all these forms of peer pressure can derail you from your future goals. Love yourself. Loving yourself will keep you from letting so-called friends influence you to do wrong. It's important that you think about your future, and pursue a path that will lead to a positive future for you, and perhaps your own future family.

Know that racism and discrimination exist; yet you do not have to let the hatred or prejudices of others stop you from being successful. Strive to be the best person you can be, in your school and in your community; and if you do that, then I assure you opportunities will follow.

Doing well in school is essential. Don't take short-cuts with your studies or let anyone rob you of a solid education by giving you a passing grade in a class when you know you don't deserve it. You owe it to yourself to take responsibility for your learning and to ensure that you are getting the full benefit of your high school and college education.

Learn to think critically, communicate effectively, and be able to perform mathematics. I know from years of experience that these are skills that will, for instance, enable you to get a good job, or be the entrepreneur who is a job creator.

A note to parents:

It's important to understand the steps that lead to college. The information contained in *Expanding College Opportunity* can assist you in guiding and supporting your child as he or she progresses through high school. Given the media hype around going to the "right" school or a highly selective college, parents can easily lose focus on the fact that your middle school or high school student is still an adolescent and likewise is developing as a young adult. (I'm a parent and I can attest to this point.) The middle school and high school years are a great time to build on your relationship with your child. Bonding is important. The time will come when your child may move across state or across country or out of the country to attend college. You'll miss your son or daughter. So then, I encourage you to enjoy your time with your student. If you follow the steps outlined in this book, your child will be on a solid path toward college and you will not have to worry about the admissions process. Your energy can remain on building on the relationship with your child.

Special note to international students:

The information contained in *Expanding College Opportunity* is relevant to both U.S. students and international students. However, there are a few points that you, as an international student, should focus on.

Ensure that your academic record is presented in such a way that an American college will understand the information. In some cases, you may need to translate your academic record into English, or provide supplemental information to ensure that colleges understand your high school program.

If you plan to study in the U.S., it is essential that your English language skills are strong. For students who apply to U.S. schools from non-English speaking countries, you will typically have to take the Test of English as a Foreign Language, T.O.E.F. L. (www.ets.org/toefl) or the International English Language Testing System exam, IELTS (www.ielts.org). In addition to earning a high enough score on the T.O.E.F.L. or IELTS exam to satisfy a college's admissions requirements, I strongly suggest that international students invest in supplemental coursework to strengthen their English reading and writing skills. As I mentioned earlier in the book, writing skills in particular are an integral component of undergraduate programs. The better you write, the easier your coursework will be.

As an international student, you might find that getting financial aid is a challenge. Many public colleges do not offer financial aid to international students. On the other hand, private colleges tend to have more flexibility in offering financial aid. Do your research to identify public and private schools that provide aid to international students. Many schools are especially welcoming of international students, as admissions officers seek to recruit a globally diverse student population.

AFTERWORD

my story

I grew up hearing many expressions about education:

- You need a degree
- Nobody can ever take your education from you
- Get that paper
- Go to school to get a good job

There is truth in these expressions. And while the expressions have a different meaning to different people, I can easily say that these expressions have meaning to me.

I think back on when I left my hometown of Dallas, Texas to attend Amherst. Going away to college was an exciting and scary experience. I had grown up in a household headed by my single mom. I went across the country to a college in a part of the United States that seemed like a foreign land.

My college years were not easy. I felt prepared academically, but I struggled to figure out how to be successful in college. I remember feeling frustrated and not clear about what to do or how to make things work. Fortunately, I was in a small enough school environment that I—through my own effort to reach out for help—was able to find the support I needed. For illustrative purposes, I want to share a few examples of the people who helped me along the way.

My college advisor, the late John A. Petropulos (1929-1999), was a major source of support. Professor Petropulos provided a "safe-haven" for me. I could go to him and talk freely about whatever was on my mind. I especially enjoyed stopping by his office on the ground floor of Amherst's Chapin Hall on Friday afternoons to chat about the week and to have what I now describe as a weekly check-in with him. Professor Petropulos or John, as he later asked me to call him, was like a father.

I also formed strong bonds with many of the College's Deans on campus, especially Dean Onawumi Jean Moss. Dean Moss was so instrumental in helping me to find a sense of place in the Amherst College community. Thanks to Dean Moss, I developed a greater sense of self-confidence. I was able to embrace the blessing of being a student at such a prestigious college, with all its history and renowned alumni, and at the same time not feel crushed by the weight of its reputation. I was and am to this day a part of the Amherst College institution. I brought my unique background and experience to the college. I had a rightful place at the school.

And finally, I sought guidance and advice from many of the college officials and administrators on campus. Amherst's Chief

Financial Officer and Treasurer, James "Jim" Scott, a former Wall Street Investment Banker, became a trusted mentor and life-long friend. Thanks to Jim's support and encouragement, I later joined the Peace Corps a few years after I graduated from college. The Peace Corps enabled me to serve as a volunteer in West Africa, but moreover the Peace Corps provided an entrée for me to see and experience the world outside the United States. I could write a book about my Peace Corps experiences alone. But the main point of my talking about the Peace Corps experience reflects back on the relationship I formed with Jim Scott and others when I was a college student. A large part of going to college, particularly traditional four-year colleges, is the growth that can come from interacting and building relationships with professors and students from all over the world.

I take the time now to mention Professor John A. Petropulos, Dean Onawumi Jean Moss, and Jim Scott because I want to acknowledge the sense of love and support they showed toward me as a young college student. Additionally, I want to point out that you (students) can always find people in a community who will help you. You are not alone. Sometimes, you just have to be courageous enough to reach out to people for help, and likewise, be humble enough to receive the help. Remember that there are lots of people who want you to be successful and will take joy in making that happen.

My College Graduation

I felt a tremendous sense of accomplishment in graduating from Amherst College. I made a contribution to Amherst through my participation in classes and through my involvement in extracurricular activities while in college. I co-founded the Black Business Association of Amherst College and was voted, from a campus wide election, to serve as our student government Treasurer.

I think that, in large part, because of my perseverance and growth as a college student, the Amherst College administration sought to recognize me and my family by inviting my mom to serve as the Honorary Marshal at my college graduation. My mom led the graduating class during the Commencement processional. She sat on stage with the Amherst College President, Trustees, and Honorary Degree Recipients. I remember her standing at the microphone with such pride, as she both opened and closed the graduation ceremonies.

Having my mom, who never went to college, serve as the Honorary Grand Marshal at my Amherst graduation might be considered by some as a small though nice gesture; but, for me, having my mother, brother, and father with me at my graduation represented the perfect culmination of my years of struggle and accomplishment. My Amherst College graduation was one of the happiest days of my life.

My mother—Rue Dean Lemons, Honorary Marshal, Amherst College 167th Commencement

Left to right: Michael Davis, me, and Zachary Gaulkin. Michael and I attended Greenhill School in Dallas, Texas. We shared many fun times together as high school friends. I met Zachary "Zack" Gaulkin, a Harvard student, during the summer after my sophomore year in college. I could not afford to travel home to Texas for the Thanksgiving holidays. Zack invited me on two occasions to spend Thanksgiving with his family in New Jersey and New Hampshire. The Gaulkins welcomed me into their family.

Life after college

After college, I worked as a Coro Foundation fellow in St. Louis, Missouri. I learned about government and business through my job assignments with the Coro Foundation. After completing my Coro Foundation fellowship, I volunteered to serve as a Peace Corps Volunteer. (Jim Scott, the Amherst College Treasurer whom I mentioned earlier had been a Peace Corps volunteer and encouraged me to join the Peace Corps.) I moved to West Africa and worked as a small business volunteer. My Peace Corps experience was incredible. I had never traveled or lived outside of the United States. It was an amazing, eye-opening experience to live and work in another country.

When I returned to the United States after serving as a Peace Corps volunteer, I moved to California to attend graduate school at the UCLA Anderson School of Business. I earned a Master of Business Administration degree (M.B.A.). I later worked in the corporate world for many large and small companies, including Citigroup, The Coca-Cola Company, and my own entrepreneurial ventures.

Throughout my professional career, I have been able to work and travel to countries around the world: Argentina, Austria, Belize, Cameroon, Ecuador, Equatorial Guinea, France, Germany, Guatemala, Hong Kong, Indonesia, Italy, Kenya, Mexico, Poland, Singapore, Spain, Slovakia, Taiwan, Tanzania, and Zanzibar. As a kid growing up in Dallas, Texas, I never imagined that I would have the opportunity to travel to all these countries.

My education propelled me. My college and graduate school experiences served to develop my analytical and communication skills. These skills have been invaluable, personally and professionally. The core skills that I learned in college continue to be a foundation for the things that I do today. I am so grateful for my education.

Has my life included ups and downs? Yes, absolutely. I too have had my share of adversity: unemployment, divorce, and illness. I am not immune to life's difficult moments.

Still, as I look back on my life thus far, I can easily say that my education, coupled with my faith, was and continues to be at the center of my ability to navigate through life's twists and turns. You might say I learned to think my way through many problems and issues.

Going to college can be in so many ways an extraordinary experience. Discoveries in science, the beauty of the performing arts, and the stimulation of intellectual discourse can all be found on college campuses. I sincerely believe that getting as much education as you can rests at the core of moving individuals forward, as well as advancing our society as a whole. I say to you, "Go for it!" Go get your degree. But after you graduate from college or graduate school, please remember to help and mentor someone else along the way.

I leave you with words that were included in my letter of acceptance to Amherst College. The incoming President, Peter R. Pouncey, described college as a place to discover "how, out of the ruck of ordinariness, against the odds and often in the midst of social turmoil and oppression, time and again an individual mind can make an extraordinary assertion, and produce a work which dominates the imagination of the world and even changes the course of its history."

I wish you all the best on **your** road to college and beyond.

Stan

"Getting that paper" (my college diploma) from Peter Pouncey, president emeritus of Amherst College

RESOURCES

top ten take-aways from
Expanding College Opportunity

1. Graduate from high school and pursue higher education.

2. Perform well in your classes.

3. Develop your reading, writing, and mathematics skills.

4. Make a positive contribution to your community.

5. Seek a good college fit.

6. Apply to a range or "basket" of colleges.

7. Save for college.

8. Complete the FAFSA and, if necessary, the CSS PROFILE.

9. Prepare a thoughtful and well-written college application.

10. Cherish your family and friends.

Bonus

Help another student on the road to college.

KEY WEBSITES

from Expanding College Opportunity

• **College Choice** • **Majors** • **Careers**	www.bigfuture.collegeboard.org www.collegeweeklive.com www.nces.ed.gov/collegenavigator
• **Financial Aid** • **Scholarships**	https://bigfuture.collegeboard.org/ scholarship-search www.fastweb.com www.finaid.org www.nasfaa.org http://knowhow2go.acenet.edu www.savingforcollege.com www.scholarships.com www.studentaid.gov
• **College Admissions Essays**	www.thesecrettowriting.com
• **Standardized Tests**	www.act.org www.collegeboard.org
• **Writing Skills**	www.thesecrettowriting.com
• **College Fairs**	www.nacacnet.org

SOURCES

Antonoff, Steven R. *College Match: A blueprint for choosing the best school for you.* Alexandria, VA: Octameron Associates. 2012.

Black, Isaac. *African American Student's College Guide.* New York, NY: John Wiley & Sons, Inc. 2000.

Kantrowitz, Mark. *Secrets to winning a scholarship.* Chicago, IL: FastWeb, LLC. 2011.

Kramer, Stephen and Michael London. *The New Rules of College Admissions: Ten former admissions officers reveal what it takes to get into college today.* New York, NY: Fireside. 2006.

Mamlet, Robin and Christine Vandevelde. *College Admission: From Application to Acceptance, Step by Step.* New York, NY: Three Rivers Press. 2011.

McGinty, Sarah Myers. *The College Application Essay.* New York, NY: The College Board. 2012.

Ostrum, Eva. *The Thinking Parent's Guide to College Admissions: The step-by-step program to get kids into the schools of their dreams.* New York, NY: Peguin Books. 2006.

Springer, Sally P., Jon Reider, and Joyce Vining Morgan. *Admission Matters.* San Francisco, CA: Jossey-Bass. 2013.

Stack, Carol and Ruth Vedvik. *Financial Aid Handbook.* Pompton Plains, NJ: The Career Press, Inc. 2011.

The Staff of The Princeton Review, *Cracking College Admissions.* New York, NY: Princeton Review Publishing, L.L.C. 2004.

ACT
www.act.org

American Association
of Community Colleges
www.aacc.nche.edu

College Board
www.collegeboard.org

College Week Live
www.collegeweeklive.com

FairTest
www.fairtest.org

Fastweb
www.fastweb.com

Federal Student Aid
www.studentaid.ed.gov

Federal Student Aid
YouTube Channel
https://www.youtube.com/user/
FederalStudentAid

Finaid
www.finaid.org

Free Application
for Federal Student Aid
www.fafsa.ed.gov

IELTS
www.ielts.org

National Association
for College Admission Counseling
www.nacacnet.org

National Association of Student
Financial Aid Administrators
www.nasfaa.org

National Center
for Education Statistics
www.nces.ed.gov/ipeds/datacenter

National College Access Network
www.collegeaccess.org

National Merit Scholarship
Corporation
www.nationalmerit.org

KnowHow2Go
knowhow2go.acenet.edu

Project GRAD Atlanta
www.atlanta.projectgrad.org

QuestBridge
www.questbridge.org

Savingforcollege.com
www.savingforcollege.com

Scholarships.com
www.scholarships.com

The Common Application
www.commonapp.org

The Gates Millennium Scholars
www.gmsp.org

The Posse Foundation, Inc.
www.possefoundation.org

TOEFL
www.ets.org/toefl

Universal College Application
www.universalcollegeapp.com